ATARI 130XE GAMES BOOK

ATARI 130XE GAMES BOOK

Richard Woolcock
&
Graeme Stretton

MELBOURNE HOUSE
PUBLISHERS

First Published in 1985 by Beam Software and Melbourne House

This Remastered Edition
Published by
Acorn Books
www.acornbooks.co.uk

Copyright © 1985, 2021 Subvert Limited

All rights reserved. No part of this publication may be reproduced, stored in a retrieval system, or transmitted, in any form or by any means without the prior written permission of the publisher, nor be otherwise circulated in any form of binding or cover other than that in which it is published and without a similar condition being imposed on the subsequent purchaser. Any person who does so may be liable to criminal prosecution and civil claims for damages. All trademarks remain the property of their respective owners.

This book is a page-by-page reproduction of the original 1985 edition as published by Beam Software and Melbourne House. The entirety of the book is presented with no changes, corrections nor updates to the original text, images and layout except for page 37 which has been reproduced in a similar style due to degradation of the original master; no guarantee is offered as to the accuracy of the information within.

CONTENTS

ARRANGEMENT OF PROGRAMS	1
Frequently Occurring Typing Errors with the Atari 130XE	1
Overall Advice	2
CHEXSUM	5
Why	5
When	5
How to tell if Chexsum has been entered correctly	6
Using Chexsum	7
BOMBER	9
OTHELLO	14
MOUNTAINS	20
VOGONS	25
LIFE	30
RATMAZE	35
2D MAZE	40
MINOTAUR	45
BATTLESHIP	51
CRYPT	56
DUNGEONS	61
LETRMAZE	68
BREAKIN	74
RACER	80
ROCKS	85
SNOWBALL	90
HUNTER	95
TAKEAWAY	100
SORTGAME	105
SLEFT	110
OXO	115
PING PONG	122
ROCK COLLECTOR	127
SNAKES	130

DIAMOND HUNT	134
SPACMAN	139
MAZING	144
WORMA	154
PATROL CAR	159
ROBOTS	164

ARRANGEMENT OF PROGRAMS

All the programs have been classified, explained and set out in an easy to read and enter format, with further programming suggestions and enhancements. We hope you enjoy this book and games within and continue to get the 'best' for and from your ATARI 130XE.

In the programs throughout this book, spaces have been used to aid readability. These have been placed between reserve words like PRINT, FOR, GOTO, GOSUB and between the characters in strings. It is not necessary to put them between reserve words most of the time however occasionally the machine will demand it. So if you type in a line omitting the spaces and the machine rejects it with a error, retype it with the spaces. The only time you should type a space inside of a string is when you see the * symbol. This avoids confusion.

The ATARI has a number of special graphics characters. These are obtained by pressing combinations of keys. The bulk of these characters are obtained by pressing the Control key and one of the alphabetic character keys. Inverse characters (reverse images of characters) are obtained by pressing the inverse key on the extreme bottom right hand side of the keyboard. Normal characters are restored by pressing this key once more.

Frequently occurring (and easily overlooked) typing errors with the ATARI 130XE

1. Do not confuse the letter O with the digit Ø (zero).

2. Do not confuse the capital letter I with the numeric digit 1 (one).

3. A comma and a full stop (period) are not interchangable.

4. When a colon is required do not type a semi-colon (;). These two characters are not interchangeable.

5. A double quote (") is not interchangeable with an apostrophe (').

6. Inside of character strings, spaces are mandatory if indicated by the * symbol.

7. It is important to get the number of brackets inside a BASIC formulae correct otherwise the line will be rejected. The bracket symbols are () and not [_.

8. The following characters are obtained by pressing the shift key and the numeric keys; ! " # $ % & ' @ ( )

Overall advice

If you type in a program line, press RETURN and the computer rejects it with an error message, then carefully compare the line with what's in the book. The line has been rejected because it has not been written according to the rules of BASIC. Retype the line correctly as per the book.

All BASIC program statements must be in upper case. Any reserve word in lower case will rejected as an error. Also reserve words may not be in the inverse mode.

Once you have typed in a program save a copy of it to tape or disk. Under no circumstances type in a program and RUN it without doing this first. Most of the programs in this book contain POKEs or machine language. If you make a mistake typing in a program and then RUN it, these are liable to erase your program or lock up the machine. If the error is disasterous enough, the only way to restart the machine is to switch it off and on, losing your program !!! If by some misfortune you should do this and the machine locks then press RESET. If control doesn't go back to BASIC then you have lost your program otherwise you may still have an oppotunity to save it to tape or disk.

Save a program to tape with

SAVE "C:FILENAME"

or to disk with

SAVE "D:FILENAME"

After you have typed in a program and saved it to either tape or disk, it's safe to RUN it. Unfortunately just because the computer has accepted a program line doesn't mean that it's correct. You are likely to be presented with a number of error messages the first time you try to RUN a program. To some extent this can be prevented by using CHEXSUM in the next section but even that won't solve all problems. Here is a list of the most common error messages and their probable causes.

ERROR-   17 AT LINE nnnn

This generally means that you have typed in a line, caused a syntax error and didn't notice it. When a syntax error occurs, the word ERROR- is entered into the start of the bad line. So when the ATARI tries to execute the line it finds garbage. The error is repaired by retyping in the line correctly.

ERROR-   12 AT LINE nnnn
The computer has been told to GOTO, GOSUB, ON GOSUB or ON GOTO to a line and the line didn't exist. Check that the line which has the above statements in it has the right linenumber. Then check that the line it was told to goto actually exists.

ERROR-   6 AT LINE nnnn
The computer tried to read some information from a DATA statement with a READ statement and there wasn't enough data present. The most obvious cause of this error is a mistake in the DATA statements. Carefully go through the DATA statements making sure that all numbers are right. Check to see that no full stops have been exchanged for commas and vice versa.

ERROR-   8 AT LINE nnnn
The computer tried to read information from DATA statements, was expecting numeric information and got character information instead. The solution to this problem is the same as above. Check through your data statements and make sure that all the information is correct. Also make sure that the READ statement where the error occured is correct.

ERROR-   3 AT LINE nnnn
The computer used a number which was out of range. For example a POKE statement tried to use a number which was not in the range 0-255. If a POKE statement contains a variable then print the contents of the variable and find out how it got to that value. Generally happens when a READ statement fetches an incorrect DATA statement and the computer tries to POKE the bad data. Check the DATA statement.

ERROR-   9 AT LINE nnnn
A reference was made to an array or a string and an error occured. There are various reasons why this error has occured. They are:

   * A reference was made to an array which didn't exist. There are two reasons for this; the variable in the line where the error occurred was incorrect, or the variable named in the DIM statement was incorrect. Check these two sources.

   * An array reference was incorrect. It was either greater than 32767 or a negative number. Check that the array reference was in this range or was not greater than the dimension size.

* A string variable must be declared with a DIM statement at the start of the program. If you get an array error for a string then either the string variable where the error occurred is wrong or the varaible in the DIM statement is wrong. When you have typed in a program and you can't get it running properly, even after numerous debugging attempts, then put the job at rest for a day or so. It often happens that you will find the bug at once after resuming the job.

CHEXSUM

The unique CHEXSUM program validation

WHY

When a book of programs such as this book is keyed in, everybody invariably makes reading and typing mistakes and then spends ages trying to sort out where and what is causing the error (errors).

Even experienced programmers often cannot identify an error just by listing the relevant line and need to do the tedious job of going back to the book, especially with DATA statements.

Realizing that this is a major cause of frustration in keying the program, we decided to do something about it. There is a short routine in this book which you should key in and save BEFORE you key in any of the games programs.

Using this routine you will be able to find out if you made any keying errors at all and in which lines, before you even RUN the program. In effect this means that with this book you need not waste time looking for keying errors, you simply run the CHEXSUM routine and look at the display to identify lines containing errors. It's that easy.

The principle behind the routine is a unique check sum which is calculated on each line of the program you have keyed into the computer. Compare this chexsum value with the value for that line in the list at the end of the program listing; if they are the same the line is correct, if not there is an error in that line.

WHEN

The simplest method is to enter the CHEXSUM program in now and save a copy of it to tape or disk. To save it to disk use

    LIST "D:CHEXSUM"

To save it to tape use

    LIST "C:CHEXSUM"

The LIST command saves a copy of the CHEXSUM program to either tape or disk in ASCII. It is only possible to reload an ASCII file using:

For tape

    ENTER "C:CHEXSUM"

For Disk

ENTER "D:CHEXSUM"

You can type in the CHEXSUM program at any time, even if you have started to type in a program. You cannot, of course LOAD in CHEXSUM from tape or disk because it will erase all you have typed so far. The obvious solution is to merge the programs. The CHEXSUM program should be saved onto a separate cassette to allow easy access.

HOW CAN YOU TELL IF CHEXSUM HAS BEEN ENTERED CORRECTLY

After having keyed in CHEXSUM it is very important that you know that CHEXSUM is working perfectly. Follow these instructions:

1. Type in the CHEXSUM program and save it to disk or tape with the commands suggested above.

2. Manually compare the CHEXSUM program you have typed in with the book. Get someone to read the book out to you while you check it against whats in the computer.

3. Keep repeating steps 1 and 2 until the checksum program is perfect.

Here is a listing of CHEXSUM and instructions on it's use:

```
32000 TOTAL=0
32010 STMTAB=PEEK(136)+PEEK(137)*256
32020 NUM=PEEK(STMTAB)+PEEK(STMTAB+1)*256
32030 IF NUM=32000 THEN GOTO 32070
32040 IF PEEK(STMTAB+4)=0 THEN 32050
32041 LINETOTAL=0:? "LINE ▲NUMBER: ▲▲";NUM;" ▲=▲";
32043 FOR T=STMTAB+4 TO STMTAB+PEEK(STMTAB+2)-1
32044 LINETOTAL=LINETOTAL+PEEK(T)
32045 NEXT T
32046 TOTAL=TOTAL+LINETOTAL
32049 ? LINETOTAL
32050 STMTAB=STMTAB+PEEK(STMTAB+2)
32060 GOTO 32020
32070 ? "TOTAL ▲=▲";TOTAL
```

USING CHEXSUM

CHEXSUM is a special program which generates a unique sum for each line in a program and a grand total of all sums. After each program listing is a table of checksums. You need only compare the numbers in the CHEXSUM table for each program with those generated by CHEXSUM. If two numbers differ, check that particular line.

1. Type in your game program, PINGPONG, say. Save it to tape or disk.

2. If you have just typed in a program then ignore this step otherwise LOAD in you game from tape or disk.

3. Merge the CHEXSUM program onto the end of your program. Do this by putting the tape or disk containing the chexsum program into the drive and for disk typing:

   ENTER "D:CHEXSUM"

for tape type:

   ENTER "C:CHEXSUM"

4. Once the CHEXSUM program has been merged onto the end of your game program, enter GOTO 32000 to activate CHEXSUM.

5. Chexsum will now output the checksum for the program. To halt the program press the Control and the '1' keys. Press again to restart output.

6. Check your grand total with that in the book. If they differ a line has been entered incorrectly. Compare line numbers until you locate the bad ones and then edit them.

7. Repeat steps 4 to 6 until the games program is debugged.

8. When the games program is running satisfactorily, delete the Chexsum program from the end of your game.

9. Finally save the debugged version onto a tape or disk.

BOMBER

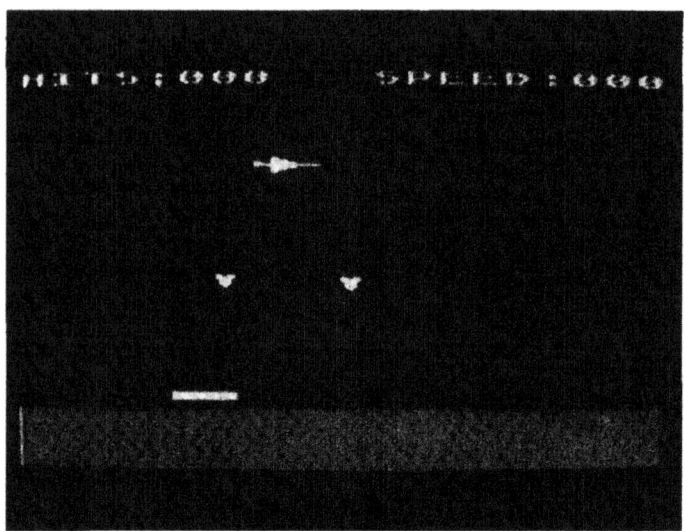

CLASSIFICATION: Skill

A plane is flying above and periodically dropping bombs on the cities below. You have a shield which you must use to explode the bombs with before they hit the ground. The longer the game runs the faster the bomber flies and the faster the bombs are dropped. After a hundred bombs are dropped the speed decreases and after a hundred catches the speed increases. Use joystick one to move the shield left and right.

PROGRAMMING SUGGESTIONS

Have more than one bomber flying overhead and increase the number of bombs that can be dropped.

Program
Variables

I	General purpose variable
PMBASE	Pointer to player missile data
PM	Page pointer to player missile data
A	Holds data begin read from data statement

Program
Structure

```
   5 -    8 Clear memory and read in programs
  10 -   85 Set up graphics mode
 100 -  120 Data for players
1000        Call machine langugae program
5000 - 5410 Data for machine language program
```

Listing

```
5       FOR I=33792 TO 33792+1023:POKE I,0:NEXT I
7       FOR I=30720 TO 30720+78:READ A:POKE I,A:NEXT I
8       FOR I=28672 TO 29510:READ A:POKE I,A:NEXT I
10      POKE 106,128
20      PM=PEEK(106):PMBASE=PM*256
30      GRAPHICS 1
35      PRINT #6;"CAUGHT:▲▲▲▲HITS:"
40      POKE 559,62
50      POKE 53277,3
60      POKE 54279,PM
70      POKE 53256,2:POKE 53257,2
80      POKE 704,77:POKE 705,88:POKE 706,88
85      POKE 707,88
100     DATA 0,32,48,184,255,56,48,32,0,0,0,0,0,0,0,0,0,0,0,0
110     DATA 255,255,255,0,0,0,0,0,0,0,0,0,0,0,0,0,0,0,0,0
115     DATA 0,0,123,255,255,123,0,0,0,0,0,0,0,0,0,0,0,0,0,0
120     DATA 0,0,123,255,255,123,0,0,0,0,0,0,0,0,0,0,0,0,0,0
1000    A=USR(112*256)
5000    DATA 32,27,112,32,72,112,32,151,112,32,41,113,32,239,11
        3,32,75,113,32,131
5010    DATA 113,32,206,113,76,3,112,169,0,141,5,115,169,50,141
        ,4,115,169,8,141
5020    DATA 7,115,169,50,141,19,115,169,150,141,18,115,169,0,1
        41,62,115,141,63,115
5030    DATA 141,66,115,141,56,115,169,5,141,65,115,96,173,60,1
        15,240,4,206,60,115
5040    DATA 96,173,65,115,141,60,115,173,7,115,201,4,240,5,201
        ,8,240,26,96,173
5050    DATA 5,115,240,4,206,5,115,96,169,8,141,7,115,32,127,11
        3,201,100,176,249
5060    DATA 141,4,115,96,173,5,115,201,163,240,4,238,5,115,96,
        169,4,141,7,115
5070    DATA 32,127,113,201,100,176,249,141,4,115,96,173,59,115
        ,240,4,206,59,115,96
5080    DATA 173,65,115,141,59,115,173,62,115,201,1,240,6,32,19
        7,112,76,182,112,32
5090    DATA 247,112,173,63,115,201,1,240,4,32,222,112,96,32,16
        ,113,96,32,127,113
5100    DATA 201,210,176,17,169,1,141,62,115,173,5,115,141,33,1
        15,173,4,115,141,32
5110    DATA 115,96,32,127,113,201,200,144,17,169,1,141,63,115,
        173,5,115,141,47,115
5120    DATA 173,4,115,141,46,115,96,173,32,115,201,155,240,4,2
        38,32,115,96,169,0
5130    DATA 141,62,115,169,220,141,32,115,238,56,115,96,173,46
        ,115,201,155,240,4,238
5140    DATA 46,115,96,169,0,141,63,115,169,220,141,46,115,238,
        56,115,96,32,247,114
5150    DATA 201,4,240,5,201,8,240,12,96,173,19,115,201,0,240,3
        ,206,19,115,96
5160    DATA 173,19,115,201,163,240,3,238,19,115,96,173,13,208,
        170,41,4,208,6,138
5170    DATA 41,8,208,20,96,169,0,141,62,115,169,220,141,32,115
        ,169,0,141,30,208
```

```
5180  DATA 238,66,115,96,169,0,141,63,115,169,220,141,46,115,
      169,0,141,30,208,238
5190  DATA 66,115,96,173,10,210,96,173,66,115,32,172,113,162,
      3,160,0,189,199,113
5200  DATA 153,135,125,200,202,208,246,173,56,115,32,172,113,
      162,3,160,0,189,199,113
5210  DATA 153,144,125,200,202,208,246,96,162,3,56,160,0,253,
      202,113,144,3,200,208
5220  DATA 248,125,202,113,72,152,9,16,157,199,113,104,202,20
      8,231,96,0,0,0,1
5230  DATA 10,100,173,66,115,201,100,240,8,173,56,115,201,100
      ,240,10,96,206,65,115
5240  DATA 169,0,141,66,115,96,238,65,115,169,0,141,56,115,96
      ,120,32,202,114,160
5250  DATA 14,162,0,189,253,114,149,176,232,136,208,247,32,10
      8,114,160,14,162,0,181
5260  DATA 176,157,253,114,232,136,208,247,160,14,162,0,189,1
      1,115,149,176,232,136,208
5270  DATA 247,32,108,114,160,14,162,0,181,176,157,11,115,232
      ,136,208,247,160,14,162
5280  DATA 0,189,25,115,149,176,232,136,208,247,32,108,114,16
      0,14,162,0,181,176,157
5290  DATA 25,115,232,136,208,247,160,14,162,0,189,39,115,149
      ,176,232,136,208,247,32
5300  DATA 108,114,160,14,162,0,181,176,157,39,115,232,136,20
      8,247,32,216,114,88,96
5310  DATA 165,183,197,182,240,68,160,0,165,184,24,105,46,145
      ,176,169,32,24,101,182
5320  DATA 168,166,185,169,0,145,178,200,202,16,250,169,32,24
      ,101,183,141,64,115,162
5330  DATA 0,142,53,115,166,185,172,53,115,177,180,238,53,115
      ,172,64,115,145,178,238
5340  DATA 64,115,202,16,237,165,183,133,182,165,184,133,189,
      96,165,184,197,189,208,182
5350  DATA 96,173,57,115,41,15,170,189,230,114,238,57,115,96,
      160,14,162,0,181,176
5360  DATA 157,68,115,232,136,208,247,96,160,14,162,0,189,68,
      115,149,176,232,136,208
5370  DATA 247,96,1,2,3,4,5,10,7,8,7,8,11,4,2,4,1,4,8,173
5380  DATA 0,211,73,255,96,0,208,0,132,0,120,0,0,0,8,0,16,0,0
      ,1
5390  DATA 208,0,133,20,120,0,0,0,8,0,16,0,0,2,208,0,134,40,1
      20,0
5400  DATA 0,0,8,0,16,0,0,3,208,0,135,60,120,0,0,0,8,0,0,0
5410  DATA 0,0,0,79,0,0,0,0,0,0,0,0,0,5,0,0,0,0,156
```

ChexSum Tables

5	= 1421	5030	= 3556	5240	= 3559
7	= 1494	5040	= 3405	5250	= 3703
8	= 1568	5050	= 3450	5260	= 3866
10	= 277	5060	= 3358	5270	= 3745
20	= 1124	5070	= 3611	5280	= 3714
30	= 144	5080	= 3549	5290	= 3769
35	= 1218	5090	= 3484	5300	= 3719
40	= 420	5100	= 3533	5310	= 3726
50	= 406	5110	= 3590	5320	= 3761
60	= 473	5120	= 3507	5330	= 3776
70	= 782	5130	= 3706	5340	= 3956
80	= 1203	5140	= 3623	5350	= 3625
85	= 378	5150	= 3285	5360	= 3788
100	= 2454	5160	= 3509	5370	= 2398
110	= 2368	5170	= 3446	5380	= 2652
115	= 2372	5180	= 3616	5390	= 2736
120	= 2188	5190	= 3567	5400	= 2390
1000	= 716	5200	= 3748	5410	= 2037
5000	= 3467	5210	= 3630		
5010	= 3393	5220	= 3390		
5020	= 3601	5230	= 3619	TOTAL	= 166569

OTHELLO

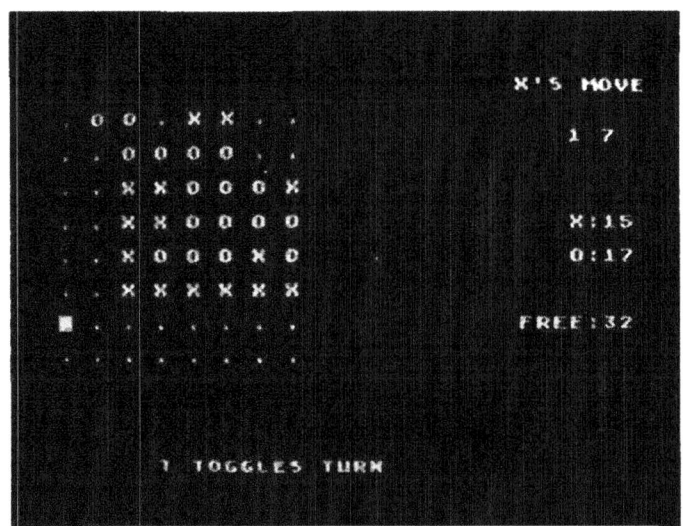

CLASSIFICATION: Strategy

This game uses the computer as a medium for two people to play the game of Othello. Pressing / or ? will display all the legal moves on the board as question marks. Placing the cursor over any man and pressing fire will do the same. If you have no legal moves then press T to change who's turn it is. Displayed on the right hand side of the screen is :

Who's turn (X or O)
The cursors current position x,y
The number of X's
The number of O's
The amount of free spaces on board

Use either joystick to move the cursor over the board. Press fire on either joystick to make a move. If you don't know how to play use ? to display legal moves and observe the results of making these moves. The object of the game is to have the most men at the end of the game. If a player has no legal moves then it becomes the other players turn to move (use T). The game is over when there are no legal moves for either player.

PROGRAMMING SUGGESTIONS

The board display could be done in high resolution with color. A command to take back the last move made would be useful. The machine could play against a human.

Program Variables

B( )	Holds the position of men on the board
C	Local variable
CURH	Cursor's horizontal position
CURV	Cursor's vertical position
LOOP	Loop counter
O	Used in count men routine
OLDCUR	Cursor's old position
P	Index to array
PH	Holds inital value of P
R	Local variable
SCREEN	Address of start of video RAM
STOR	Stores value of character under the cursor
TURN	Who's turn 1 or -1
V	Used in move cursor routine
VALID	0 if move not valid else =1
X	Local variable, in delay routine etc.
Z	Local variable
ZZ	Counter for display in find all legal moves routine

Program Structure

10	Set colors and jump to initialization
100 - 800	Make a move
1000 - 1560	Find and make legal moves
9000	Delay routine
9100	Invalid move routine
10000 - 10080	Draw the board
10100 - 10130	Count number of men
10150 - 10220	Print information
11000 - 11140	Move the cursor
12000 - 12040	Put the cursor on screen
20000 - 20030	Initialize the system
30000 - 30070	Main loop

Listing

> Set colors and jump to initialization

```
10    SETCOLOR 1,0,12:SETCOLOR 2,0,0:POKE 752,1:GOTO 20000
50    DATA -10,-9,-8,-1,1,8,9,10
```

> Make a move

```
100   IF STOR=31 THEN STOR=14
110   VALID=0:IF STOR<>14 THEN 1000
120   RESTORE 50:C=CURV:R=CURH
200   FOR LOOP=1 TO 8
210   P=R*9+C:PH=P
220   READ Z
230   P=P+Z
240   IF B(P)=0 THEN 500
250   IF B(P)=TURN THEN 500
260   P=P+Z
270   IF B(P)=0 THEN 500
280   IF B(P)=-TURN THEN GOTO 260
290   P=PH
300   VALID=1
310   B(P)=TURN
320   P=P+Z
330   IF B(P)=TURN THEN 500
340   GOTO 310
500   NEXT LOOP
600   IF NOT VALID THEN GOTO 9100
610   STOR=47:IF TURN=1 THEN STOR=56
700   TURN=-TURN
800   GOTO 30000
```

> Find and make legal moves

```
1000  POKE OLDCUR,STOR:ZZ=63:VALID=0:FOR C=1 TO 8:FOR R=1 TO
      8:RESTORE 50:POSITION 20,0:? ZZ;" ▲";:ZZ=ZZ-1
1010  P=R*9+C:IF B(P) THEN 1510
1200  FOR LOOP=1 TO 8:P=R*9+C:PH=P:READ Z:P=P+Z:IF B(P)=0 OR
      B(P)=4 THEN 1500
1250  IF B(P)=TURN THEN 1500
1270  P=P+Z:IF B(P)=0 OR B(P)=4 THEN 1500
1280  IF B(P)=-TURN THEN 1270
1310  VALID=1:B(PH)=4:LOOP=8
1500  NEXT LOOP
```

```
1510    NEXT R:NEXT C
1520    IF VALID THEN GOTO 1550
1530    POSITION 8,23:? "YOU HAVE NO MOVES";
1540    GOSUB 9000:TURN=-TURN:GOTO 30000
1550    P=CURH*9+CURV:IF B(P)=4 THEN STOR=31
1560    GOTO 30000
```

> Delay routine

```
9000    FOR X=1 TO 1000:NEXT X:RETURN
```

> Invalid move routine

```
9100    POSITION 7,23:? "▲▲";:POSITION 10,23:? "INVALID
        MOVE";:GOSUB 9000:GOTO 30000
9998    REM G.STRETTON 85
```

> Draw the board

```
10000   ? CHR$(125):?
10010   FOR C=1 TO 8:FOR R=1 TO 8:P=R*9+C:IF B(P)=4 THEN ? "?▲"
        ;:B(P)=0:NEXT R:? :? :NEXT C:GOTO 10100
10050   IF  NOT B(P) THEN ? ". ▲";:GOTO 10080
10060   IF B(P)=1 THEN ? "X▲";:NEXT R:? :? :NEXT C:GOTO 10100
10070   ? "O▲";
10080   NEXT R:? :? :NEXT C
```

> Count number of men

```
10100   X=0:O=0:FOR R=10 TO 80:IF  NOT B(R) THEN NEXT R:GOTO 10
        150
10110   IF B(R)=1 THEN X=X+1
10120   IF B(R)=-1 THEN O=O+1
10130   NEXT R
```

Print information

```
10150 POSITION 33,8:? "X:";X;
10160 POSITION 33,10:? "O:";O;
10170 POSITION 30,14:? "FREE:";64-(X+O);
10180 POSITION 30,0:IF TURN=1 THEN ? "X";
10190 IF TURN=-1 THEN ? "O";
10200 ? "'S▲MOVE";
10210 POSITION 8,23:? "T▲TOGGLES▲TURN";
10220 RETURN
```

Move the cursor

```
11000 V=STICK(0):IF V=15 THEN V=STICK(1)
11010 IF V=15 THEN RETURN
11020 IF V=14 THEN CURV=CURV-1
11030 IF V=6 THEN CURV=CURV-1:CURH=CURH+1
11040 IF V=7 THEN CURH=CURH+1
11050 IF V=5 THEN CURH=CURH+1:CURV=CURV+1
11060 IF V=13 THEN CURV=CURV+1
11070 IF V=9 THEN CURV=CURV+1:CURH=CURH-1
11080 IF V=11 THEN CURH=CURH-1
11090 IF V=10 THEN CURH=CURH-1:CURV=CURV-1
11100 IF CURH<1 THEN CURH=CURH+8
11110 IF CURH>8 THEN CURH=CURH-8
11120 IF CURV<1 THEN CURV=CURV+8
11130 IF CURV>8 THEN CURV=CURV-8
11140 RETURN
```

Put the cursor on screen

```
12000 POKE OLDCUR,STOR
12010 OLDCUR=SCREEN+(CURV*80)+(CURH*2)
12020 STOR=PEEK(OLDCUR)
12030 POKE OLDCUR,128
12040 RETURN
```

Initialize the system

```
20000 ? CHR$(125):DIM B(90):FOR X=0 TO 90:B(X)=0:NEXT X
20020 B(41)=1:B(49)=1:B(40)=-1:B(50)=-1:TURN=1
20030 SCREEN=40000:CURH=1:CURV=1:STOR=14:OLDCUR=SCREEN+(CURV*
      80)+(CURH*2)
```

> Main loop

```
30000 GOSUB 10000:REM DRAW SCREEN
30010 GOSUB 11000:REM ADJUST CURSOR
30020 GOSUB 12000:REM PUT CURSOR
30030 IF ( NOT STRIG(1)) OR ( NOT STRIG(0)) THEN 100
30040 G=PEEK(754):IF G=45 THEN POKE 754,255:TURN=-TURN:GOTO 3
      0000
30050 POSITION 33,3:? CURH;"▲";CURV;
30060 IF G=38 OR G=102 THEN POKE 754,255:GOTO 1000
30070 POKE 77,0:FOR X=1 TO 6:NEXT X:POKE OLDCUR,STOR:FOR X=1
      TO 3:NEXT X:GOTO 30010
```

ChexSum Tables

```
   10 = 1146        1500 = 173         11050 = 1407
   50 = 1162        1510 = 349         11060 = 861
  100 = 713         1520 = 400         11070 = 1412
  110 = 720         1530 = 3809        11080 = 864
  120 = 1055        1540 = 887         11090 = 1420
  200 = 407         1550 = 1705        11100 = 841
  210 = 1133        1560 = 115         11110 = 850
  220 = 201         9000 = 716         11120 = 835
  230 = 589         9100 = 4238        11130 = 844
  240 = 577        10000 = 422         11140 = 58
  250 = 710        10010 = 4227        12000 = 355
  260 = 589        10050 = 928         12010 = 1308
  270 = 577        10060 = 1539        12020 = 577
  280 = 890        10070 = 211         12030 = 339
  290 = 408        10080 = 498         12040 = 58
  300 = 337        10100 = 2185        20000 = 2254
  310 = 657        10110 = 1102        20020 = 3127
  320 = 589        10120 = 1159        20030 = 2891
  330 = 710        10130 = 171         30000 = 1077
  340 = 130        10150 = 746         30010 = 1282
  500 = 173        10160 = 746         30020 = 1085
  600 = 485        10170 = 1466        30030 = 896
  610 = 1185       10180 = 777         30040 = 2169
  700 = 469        10190 = 549         30050 = 778
  800 = 115        10200 = 570         30060 = 1295
 1000 = 3725       10210 = 1445        30070 = 2309
 1010 = 1295       10220 = 58
 1200 = 3719       11000 = 1399        TOTAL = 96503
 1250 = 726        11010 = 395
 1270 = 1773       11020 = 863
 1280 = 889        11030 = 1409
 1310 = 1347       11040 = 853
```

MOUNTAINS

CLASSIFICATION: Arcade

Fly the ship through the mountains for as long as possible without hitting the mountains. If your ship touches the mountains the hit count is incremented. Every now and again a missile will fly by and you must avoid it or the hit counter will be incremented. Move the ship using joystick port 1.

PROGRAMMING SUGGESTIONS

Increase the intelligence of the enemy missiles so that when they come hurtling across the screen they will seek your craft out. Add objects to the bottom of the landscape that you have to pick up to keep the game going. Give the player a limited amount of fuel and time to complete his journey through the mountains.

Program Variables

I	General purpose variable
PMBASE	Pointer to player/missile area
A	Dummy variable

Program Structure

```
   1 -   80 Initialize memory and variables
  90       Call machine language program
 100 -  120 Data for players
2000 - 2114 Data for machine language program
```

Listing

```
1       PRINT CHR$(125);"INITIALIZATION PLEASE WAIT"
5       FOR I=30720 TO 30720+48:READ A:POKE I,A:NEXT I
6       FOR I=28672 TO 29820:READ A:POKE I,A:NEXT I
7       FOR I=33792 TO 33792+1023:POKE I,0:NEXT I
10      POKE 106,128
20      PM=PEEK(106):PMBASE=PM*256
30      GRAPHICS 1
40      POKE 559,62
50      POKE 53277,3
60      POKE 54279,PM
70      POKE 53256,1
80      POKE 704,77:POKE 705,88:POKE 706,88
90      A=USR(112*256)
100     DATA 128,192,248,228,226,255,255,124,0,0,0,0,0,0,0,0,0,
        0,0,0
110     DATA 0,0,123,255,255,123,0,0,0,0,0,0,0,0,0,0,0,0,0,0
120     DATA 0,0,222,255,255,222,0,0,0
2000    DATA 32,30,112,32,216,113,32,138,112,32,77,114,32,169,1
        14,32,75,115,32,252
2002    DATA 114,32,18,113,238,124,116,76,3,112,169,1,141,123,1
        16,141,214,113,169,206
2004    DATA 141,88,116,169,50,141,87,116,169,0,141,74,115,141,
        73,115,133,77,141,30
2006    DATA 208,162,4,160,0,185,90,112,153,128,125,200,202,208
        ,246,162,6,160,0,185
2008    DATA 94,112,153,139,125,200,202,208,246,96,40,41,52,26,
        51,35,47,50,37,26
2010    DATA 206,127,116,96,162,3,56,160,0,253,134,112,144,3,20
        0,208,248,125,134,112
2012    DATA 72,152,9,16,157,131,112,104,202,208,231,96,0,0,0,1
        ,10,100,174,127
2014    DATA 116,208,213,162,60,142,127,116,162,0,160,19,189,14
        9,125,157,148,125,189,169
2016    DATA 125,157,168,125,189,189,125,157,188,125,189,209,12
        5,157,208,125,189,229,125,157
2018    DATA 228,125,189,249,125,157,248,125,189,13,126,157,12,
        126,189,33,126,157,32,126
2020    DATA 189,53,126,157,52,126,189,73,126,157,72,126,189,93
        ,126,157,92,126,189,113
2022    DATA 126,157,112,126,189,133,126,157,132,126,189,153,12
        6,157,152,126,189,173,126,157
2024    DATA 172,126,189,193,126,157,192,126,189,213,126,157,21
        2,126,189,233,126,157,232,126
2026    DATA 189,253,126,157,252,126,232,136,208,138,32,59,113,
        96,173,73,115,32,104,112
2028    DATA 162,3,160,0,189,131,112,153,132,125,200,202,208,24
        6,173,74,115,32,104,112
2030    DATA 162,3,160,0,189,131,112,153,145,125,200,202,208,24
        6,96,169,167,133,240,169
2032    DATA 125,133,241,160,0,162,18,169,0,145,240,169,20,24,1
        01,240,133,240,169,0
2034    DATA 101,241,133,241,202,208,236,32,176,113,174,214,113
        ,169,167,133,240,169,125,133
2036    DATA 241,160,0,169,3,145,240,165,240,24,105,20,133,240,
        169,0,101,241,133,241
```

```
2038  DATA 202,208,236,169,5,24,109,214,113,141,215,113,56,16
      9,20,237,215,113,240,31
2040  DATA 170,169,15,133,240,169,127,133,241,160,0,169,3,145
      ,240,165,240,56,233,20
2042  DATA 133,240,165,241,233,0,133,241,202,208,236,96,173,1
      0,210,170,41,1,208,17
2044  DATA 138,41,128,208,1,96,173,214,113,201,15,240,3,238,2
      14,113,96,173,214,113
2046  DATA 201,1,240,232,206,214,113,76,184,113,7,0,173,77,11
      6,13,78,116,240,12
2048  DATA 173,77,116,208,3,206,78,116,206,77,116,96,169,7,14
      1,77,116,169,0,141
2050  DATA 78,116,32,71,114,201,1,240,16,201,2,240,22,201,4,2
      40,30,201,8,240
2052  DATA 36,32,57,114,96,174,73,116,240,4,202,142,73,116,96
      ,174,73,116,224,151
2054  DATA 240,4,232,142,73,116,96,174,74,116,240,4,202,142,7
      4,116,96,174,74,116
2056  DATA 224,205,240,4,232,142,74,116,96,173,74,116,240,8,2
      06,74,116,169,20,141
2058  DATA 126,116,96,173,0,211,73,255,96,173,123,116,208,32,
      32,252,115,201,210,176
2060  DATA 3,32,93,114,96,169,1,141,123,116,32,252,115,201,15
      1,176,249,141,87,116
2062  DATA 169,206,141,88,116,96,173,91,116,13,92,116,240,12,
      173,91,116,208,3,206
2064  DATA 92,116,206,91,116,96,173,88,116,240,14,206,88,116,
      169,7,141,91,116,169
2066  DATA 0,141,92,116,96,169,0,141,123,116,169,7,141,91,116
      ,169,0,141,92,116
2068  DATA 96,173,128,116,240,4,32,205,114,96,173,132,2,240,1
      ,96,173,73,116,141
2070  DATA 101,116,173,74,116,24,105,8,141,102,116,169,1,141,
      128,116,96,173,105,116
2072  DATA 13,106,116,240,12,173,105,116,208,3,206,106,116,20
      6,105,116,96,173,102,116
2074  DATA 201,206,240,14,238,102,116,169,5,141,105,116,169,0
      ,141,106,116,96,169,0
2076  DATA 141,128,116,96,173,4,208,41,1,208,15,173,12,208,41
      ,2,208,17,173,13
2078  DATA 208,41,4,208,27,96,238,73,115,169,0,141,30,208,96,
      169,200,141,87,116
2080  DATA 141,88,116,169,0,141,123,116,32,18,115,96,169,200,
      141,87,116,141,88,116
2082  DATA 141,101,116,141,102,116,169,0,141,123,116,141,30,2
      08,141,128,116,238,74,115
2084  DATA 96,0,0,120,32,21,116,160,14,162,0,189,66,116,149,1
      76,232,136,208,247
2086  DATA 32,171,115,160,14,162,0,181,176,157,66,116,232,136
      ,208,247,160,14,162,0
2088  DATA 189,80,116,149,176,232,136,208,247,32,171,115,160,
      14,162,0,181,176,157,80
2090  DATA 116,232,136,208,247,160,14,162,0,189,94,116,149,17
      6,232,136,208,247,32,171
2092  DATA 115,160,14,162,0,181,176,157,94,116,232,136,208,24
      7,32,35,116,88,96,165
2094  DATA 183,197,182,240,68,160,0,165,184,24,105,46,145,176
      ,169,32,24,101,182,168
```

```
2096  DATA 166,185,169,0,145,178,200,202,16,250,169,32,24,101
      ,183,141,129,116,162,0
2098  DATA 142,122,116,166,185,172,122,116,177,180,238,122,11
      6,172,129,116,145,178,238,129
2100  DATA 116,202,16,237,165,183,133,182,165,184,133,189,96,
      165,184,197,189,208,182,96
2102  DATA 173,124,116,10,144,2,73,29,141,124,116,96,173,10,2
      10,173,10,210,173,10
2104  DATA 210,173,10,210,96,160,14,162,0,181,176,157,130,116
      ,232,136,208,247,96,160
2106  DATA 14,162,0,189,130,116,149,176,232,136,208,247,96,1,
      2,3,4,5,10,7
2108  DATA 8,7,8,11,4,2,4,1,4,8,0,208,0,132,0,120,0,0,0,8
2110  DATA 0,16,0,0,1,208,0,133,20,120,0,0,0,8,0,16,0,0,2,208

2112  DATA 0,134,40,120,0,0,0,8,0,16,0,0,3,208,0,135,60,120,0
      ,0
2114  DATA 0,8,0,0,0,0,0,0,79
```

ChexSum Tables

```
   1 = 2276        2020 = 3811        2072 = 3780
   5 = 1446        2022 = 4086        2074 = 3643
   6 = 1587        2024 = 4089        2076 = 3399
   7 = 1421        2026 = 3820        2078 = 3524
  10 = 277         2028 = 3724        2080 = 3667
  20 = 1124        2030 = 3807        2082 = 3824
  30 = 144         2032 = 3580        2084 = 3505
  40 = 420         2034 = 3994        2086 = 3648
  50 = 406         2036 = 3621        2088 = 3773
  60 = 473         2038 = 3741        2090 = 3822
  70 = 371         2040 = 3700        2092 = 3678
  80 = 1203        2042 = 3629        2094 = 3729
  90 = 716         2044 = 3646        2096 = 3701
 100 = 2810        2046 = 3488        2098 = 4073
 110 = 2372        2048 = 3539        2100 = 3962
 120 = 1360        2050 = 3307        2102 = 3577
2000 = 3534        2052 = 3568        2104 = 3749
2002 = 3688        2054 = 3566        2106 = 3206
2004 = 3613        2056 = 3608        2108 = 2363
2006 = 3589        2058 = 3701        2110 = 2537
2008 = 3458        2060 = 3607        2112 = 2637
2010 = 3639        2062 = 3620        2114 = 1012
2012 = 3320        2064 = 3641
2014 = 3878        2066 = 3460
2016 = 4118        2068 = 3508        TOTAL = 225500
2018 = 3892        2070 = 3695
```

VOGONS

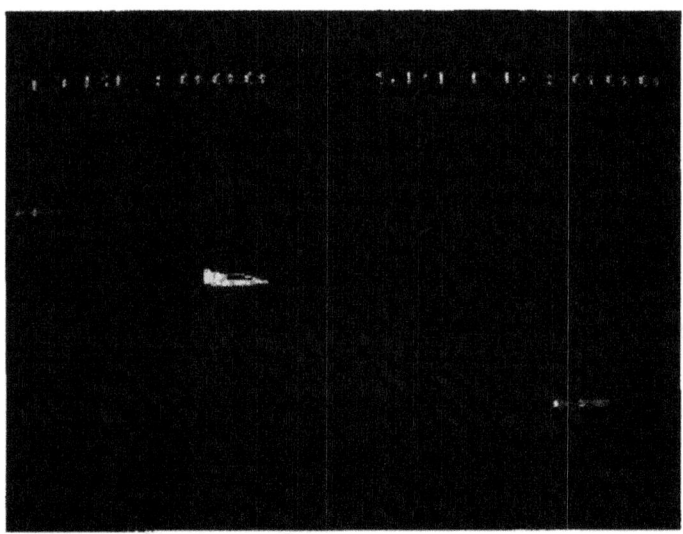

CLASSIFICATION: Skill

Move your player around the screen for as long as possible, avoiding the dreaded **Vogons**. There are three **Vogons** and they move around the screen at random, very quickly. At the start of the game you are prompted for the speed you want the **Vogons** to travel at. You may input any value between 1 and 255, with 1 being the highest speed and 255 the slowest. Use joystick 1 to move your player left, right, up and down. The longer you survive the more the score counter is incremented. When you are hit by a **Vogon** the score counter is set to zero.

PROGRAMMING SUGGESTIONS

Plant mines on the screen to restrict the area your player can move in and add 'bombs' that will disable or freeze your movement temporarily.

Program Variables

I	General purpose variable
PMBASE	Location of player missle data
PM	Pointer to player missile data
A	Holds data read from data statements

Program Structure

1 -	6	Clear the player area and read data
10 -	85	Setup the player missiles
90		Call machine language program
100 -	130	Data for players
5000 -	5460	Data for machine language program

Listing

```
1    FOR I=33792 TO 33792+1023:POKE I,0:NEXT I
5    FOR I=30720 TO 30720+79:READ A:POKE I,A:NEXT I
6    FOR I=28672 TO 29600:READ A:POKE I,A:NEXT I
10   POKE 106,128
20   PM=PEEK(106):PMBASE=PM*256
25   PRINT CHR$(125);:PRINT "WHAT SPEED ";
26   INPUT A:IF A<1 OR A>9 THEN GOTO 26
27   POKE 29595,A
30   GRAPHICS 1
35   POSITION 0,0:PRINT #6;"TIME:      SPEED:"
40   POKE 559,62
50   POKE 53277,3
60   POKE 54279,PM
70   POKE 53256,3:POKE 53257,3:POKE 53258,3:POKE 53259,3
80   POKE 704,77:POKE 705,88:POKE 706,88
85   POKE 707,77
90   A=USR(112*256)
```

Data for players

```
100  DATA 128,192,248,228,226,255,255,124,0,0,0,0,0,0,0,0,0,0,
     0,0,0
110  DATA 0,0,123,255,255,123,0,0,0,0,0,0,0,0,0,0,0,0,0
120  DATA 0,0,222,255,255,222,0,0,0,0,0,0,0,0,0,0,0,0,0
130  DATA 0,0,222,255,255,222,0,0,0,0,0,0,0,0,0,0,0,0,0
```

Data for machine language program

```
5000 DATA 32,21,112,32,169,112,32,253,112,32,101,114,32,44,1
     14,32,87,112,76,3
5010 DATA 112,169,0,141,143,115,169,50,141,91,115,141,90,115
     ,169,8,141,107,115,169
5020 DATA 0,141,105,115,169,50,140,104,115,169,50,141,119,11
     5,141,118,115,169,2,141
5030 DATA 121,115,169,25,141,133,115,141,132,115,169,4,141,1
     35,115,169,0,141,149,115
5040 DATA 141,148,115,141,30,208,96,173,149,115,13,150,115,2
     40,20,56,173,149,115,233
5050 DATA 1,141,149,115,173,150,115,233,0,141,150,115,76,128
     ,112,169,0,141,149,115
5060 DATA 169,3,141,150,115,238,148,115,173,148,115,32,61,11
     4,162,3,160,0,189,88
5070 DATA 114,153,133,125,200,202,208,246,173,155,115,32,61,
     114,162,3,160,0,189,88
5080 DATA 114,153,144,125,200,202,208,246,96,173,94,115,240,
     4,206,94,115,96,169,3
5090 DATA 141,94,115,32,95,114,170,41,1,208,16,138,41,2,208,
     23,138,41,4,208
5100 DATA 30,138,41,8,208,35,96,173,90,115,201,8,208,1,96,20
```

```
      6,90,115,96,173
5110  DATA 90,115,201,153,208,1,96,238,90,115,96,173,91,115,2
      08,1,96,206,91,115
5120  DATA 96,173,91,115,201,130,208,1,96,238,91,115,96,173,1
      42,115,240,4,206,142
5130  DATA 115,96,173,155,115,141,142,115,173,105,115,141,146
      ,115,173,104,115,141,147,115
5140  DATA 173,107,115,141,145,115,173,152,115,141,151,115,32
      ,166,113,173,151,115,141,152
5150  DATA 115,173,145,115,141,107,115,173,146,115,141,105,11
      5,173,147,115,141,104,115,173
5160  DATA 119,115,141,146,115,173,118,115,141,147,115,173,12
      1,115,141,145,115,173,153,115
5170  DATA 141,151,115,32,166,113,173,151,115,141,153,115,173
      ,145,115,141,121,115,173,146
5180  DATA 115,141,119,115,173,147,115,141,118,115,173,133,11
      5,141,146,115,173,132,115,141
5190  DATA 147,115,173,135,115,141,145,115,173,154,115,141,15
      1,115,32,166,113,173,151,115
5200  DATA 141,154,115,173,145,115,141,135,115,173,146,115,14
      1,133,115,173,147,115,141,132
5210  DATA 115,96,173,145,115,201,1,240,13,201,2,240,32,201,4
      ,240,51,201,8,240
5220  DATA 68,96,173,151,115,240,10,206,151,115,173,147,115,2
      01,8,208,4,32,20,114
5230  DATA 96,206,147,115,96,173,151,115,240,14,206,151,115,1
      73,147,115,201,153,240,4
5240  DATA 238,147,115,96,32,20,114,96,173,151,115,240,12,206
      ,151,115,173,146,115,240
5250  DATA 4,206,146,115,96,32,20,114,96,173,151,115,240,14,2
      06,151,115,173,146,115
5260  DATA 201,130,240,4,238,146,115,96,32,20,114,96,174,10,2
      10,224,4,176,249,189
5270  DATA 79,115,141,145,115,173,10,210,201,30,144,249,141,1
      51,115,96,173,12,208,41
5280  DATA 14,208,1,96,169,0,141,148,115,141,30,208,96,162,3,
      56,160,0,253,91
5290  DATA 114,144,3,200,208,248,125,91,114,72,152,9,16,157,8
      8,114,104,202,208,231
5300  DATA 96,0,0,0,1,10,100,173,0,211,73,255,96,120,32,51,11
      5,160,14,162
5310  DATA 0,189,83,115,149,176,232,136,208,247,32,226,114,16
      0,14,162,0,181,176,157
5320  DATA 83,115,232,136,208,247,160,14,162,0,189,97,115,149
      ,176,232,136,208,247,32
5330  DATA 226,114,160,14,162,0,181,176,157,97,115,232,136,20
      8,247,160,14,162,0,189
5340  DATA 111,115,149,176,232,136,208,247,32,226,114,160,14,
      162,0,181,176,157,111,115
5350  DATA 232,136,208,247,160,14,162,0,189,125,115,149,176,2
      32,136,208,247,32,226,114
5360  DATA 160,14,162,0,181,176,157,125,115,232,136,208,247,3
      2,65,115,88,96,165,183
5370  DATA 197,182,240,68,160,0,165,184,24,105,46,145,176,169
      ,32,24,101,182,168,166
5380  DATA 185,169,0,145,178,200,202,16,250,169,32,24,101,183
      ,141,144,115,162,0,142
5390  DATA 139,115,166,185,172,139,115,177,180,238,139,115,17
```

```
           2,144,115,145,178,238,144,115
5400  DATA 202,16,237,165,183,133,182,165,184,133,189,96,165,
           184,197,189,208,182,96,160
5410  DATA 14,162,0,181,176,157,156,115,232,136,208,247,96,16
           0,14,162,0,189,156,115
5420  DATA 149,176,232,136,208,247,96,1,2,4,8,0,208,0,132,0,1
           20,0,0,0
5430  DATA 8,0,16,0,0,1,208,0,133,20,120,0,0,0,8,0,16,0,0,2
5440  DATA 208,0,134,40,120,0,0,0,8,0,16,0,0,3,208,0,135,60,1
           20,0
5450  DATA 0,0,8,0,0,0,0,0,79,0,0,0,0,0,0,0,0,0,0
5460  DATA 0,0,0,0,0,0,4,33,0
```

ChexSum Tables

1 = 1421	5030 = 3790	5270 = 3739
5 = 1495	5040 = 3800	5280 = 3357
6 = 1553	5050 = 3686	5290 = 3649
10 = 277	5060 = 3613	5300 = 3168
20 = 1124	5070 = 3694	5310 = 3719
25 = 1230	5080 = 3666	5320 = 3777
26 = 931	5090 = 3347	5330 = 3712
27 = 580	5100 = 3375	5340 = 3847
30 = 144	5110 = 3521	5350 = 3863
35 = 1328	5120 = 3611	5360 = 3727
40 = 420	5130 = 3991	5370 = 3730
50 = 406	5140 = 3981	5380 = 3691
60 = 473	5150 = 4035	5390 = 4087
70 = 1663	5160 = 4039	5400 = 3961
80 = 1203	5170 = 3981	5410 = 3719
85 = 361	5180 = 4035	5420 = 2981
90 = 716	5190 = 3989	5430 = 2439
100 = 2810	5200 = 4036	5440 = 2743
110 = 2372	5210 = 3412	5450 = 2024
120 = 2372	5220 = 3591	5460 = 998
130 = 2372	5230 = 3799	
5000 = 3424	5240 = 3798	
5010 = 3704	5250 = 3696	TOTAL = 193135
5020 = 3733	5260 = 3606	

LIFE

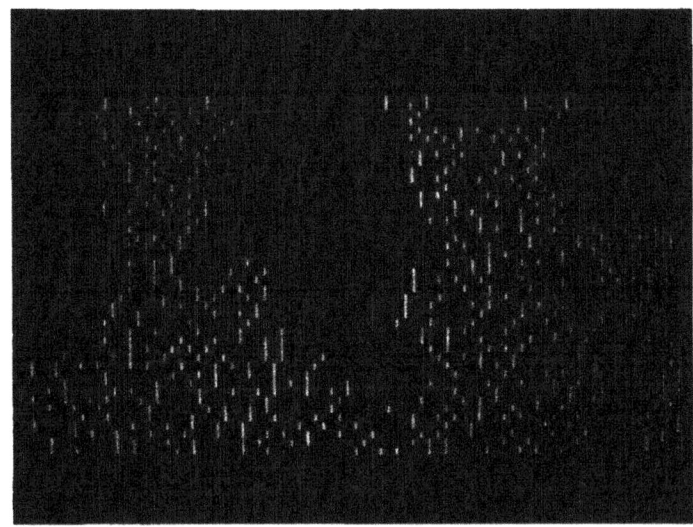

CLASSIFICATION: Educational

Life is a simulation of the growth of a colony of cells that is controlled by prescribed rules. The joystick moves the cursor left and right. Pressing the fire button on the joystick sets the cell to the current cursor color. Pressing the R key sets a random starting pattern. Pressing the ESC key changes the cursor color and pressing RETURN exits the setup stage and starts the simulation.

PROGRAMMING SUGGESTIONS

Change the radius of the neighbourhood and change the rules that drive the game.

Program Variables

```
OLDCELLS( )    Holds current array of cells
NUCELLS( )     Working copy of cells
R( )           Rule table
R              Radius of neighbourhood
K              Number of possible states of a cell
```

Program Structure

```
    10             Jump to initialization
   100 -    170   Main Loop
  5000            Display
  6000 -   6080   Calculate next generation
  9000            Random setup
 20000 -  20030   Initialize routine
 20050 -  20076   Set number of states
 20400 -  23010   Setup initial formation
```

31

Listing

```
10      GOTO 20000
```

> Main Loop

```
100     POKE 77,0:OLDCELLS(81)=OLDCELLS(1):OLDCELLS(0)=OLDCELLS
        (80)
140     T=USR(1536):REM SCROLL SCREEN
150     GOSUB 5000:REM DISPLAY
160     GOSUB 6000:REM CALC NEXT GENERATION
170     GOTO 100
```

> Display

```
5000    POSITION 0,OFFSET:FOR T=1 TO 80:? #6;CHR$(OLDCELLS(T));
        :NEXT T:RETURN
```

> Calculate next generation

```
6000    FOR I=1 TO 80
6010    S=0:FOR P=I-R TO I+R
6020    Z=P:IF Z>80 THEN Z=Z-80
6030    IF Z<1 THEN Z=Z+80
6040    S=S+OLDCELLS(Z)
6050    NEXT P
6060    NUCELLS(I)=R(S)
6070    NEXT I
6080    FOR I=1 TO 80:OLDCELLS(I)=NUCELLS(I):NEXT I:RETURN
```

> Random setup

```
9000    FOR I=1 TO 80:OLDCELLS(I)=INT(RND(0)*K):NEXT I:DSPFLAG=
        1:RETURN
20000   DIM OLDCELLS(81),NUCELLS(81)
20030   GOSUB 30000
```

> Initialize routine

```
20050   K=2:REM NUMBER OF POSSIBLE STATES
20060   R=2:REM RADIUS OF NEIGHBOURHOOD
20062   DIM R(5)
```

> Set number of states

```
20071 R(0)=0
20072 R(1)=0
20073 R(2)=1
20074 R(3)=0
20075 R(4)=1
20076 R(5)=0
```

> Setup initial formation

```
20400 FOR T=0 TO 81:OLDCELLS(T)=0
20410 NEXT T
21000 GRAPHICS 5
21010 X=40:? "R=RND..RETURN=START.JSTK.MOVES.CURSOR";? "Esc=C
      OLOUR"
21020 COLR=1
21030 OFFSET=0
21040 IF DSPFLAG THEN GOSUB 5000
21050 A=STICK(1):OLDX=X:DSPFLAG=0
21060 IF A=11 THEN X=X-1:IF X<0 THEN X=X+80
21070 IF A=7 THEN X=X+1:IF X>79 THEN X=X-80
21090 POSITION OLDX,1:? #6,CHR$(0);
21100 POSITION X,1:? #6;CHR$(COLR);
21110 IF  NOT STRIG(1) THEN OLDCELLS(X+1)=COLR:DSPFLAG=1
21130 A=PEEK(764):POKE 764,255
21140 IF A=28 THEN COLR=COLR+1:IF COLR>K-1 THEN COLR=0
21150 IF A=40 THEN GOSUB 9000
22000 IF A<>12 THEN GOTO 21040
23000 GRAPHICS 5+16:REM G.STRETTON 85
23010 OFFSET=47:GOTO 100
30000 FOR T=1536 TO 1601:READ A:POKE T,A:NEXT T:RETURN
31000 DATA 104,169,47,141,66,6,169,160,133,203,169,155,133,20
      4,169,180,133,205,169,155
31001 DATA 133,206,160,0,162,20,177,205,145,203,200,202,208,2
      48,165,203,24,105,20
31002 DATA 133,203,169,0,101,204,133,204,165,205,24,105,20,13
      3,205,169,0,101,206
31003 DATA 133,206,206,66,6,208,213,96
```

ChexSum Tables

```
   10 = 114           20050 = 5682        21090 = 741
  100 = 2084          20060 = 5283        21100 = 869
  140 = 1705          20062 = 370         21110 = 1531
  150 = 903           20071 = 393         21130 = 1085
  160 = 1804          20072 = 458         21140 = 1753
  170 = 112           20073 = 524         21150 = 641
 5000 = 1934          20074 = 460         22000 = 528
 6000 = 523           20075 = 526         23000 = 1376
 6010 = 1172          20076 = 462         23010 = 542
 6020 = 1521          20400 = 998         30000 = 1404
 6030 = 964           20410 = 166         31000 = 3877
 6040 = 814           21000 = 148         31001 = 3575
 6050 = 171           21010 = 4206        31002 = 3518
 6060 = 885           21020 = 348         31003 = 1496
 6070 = 169           21030 = 272
 6080 = 1736          21040 = 390
 9000 = 2357          21050 = 1288        TOTAL = 68830
20000 = 955           21060 = 1852
20030 = 117           21070 = 2028
```

RATMAZE

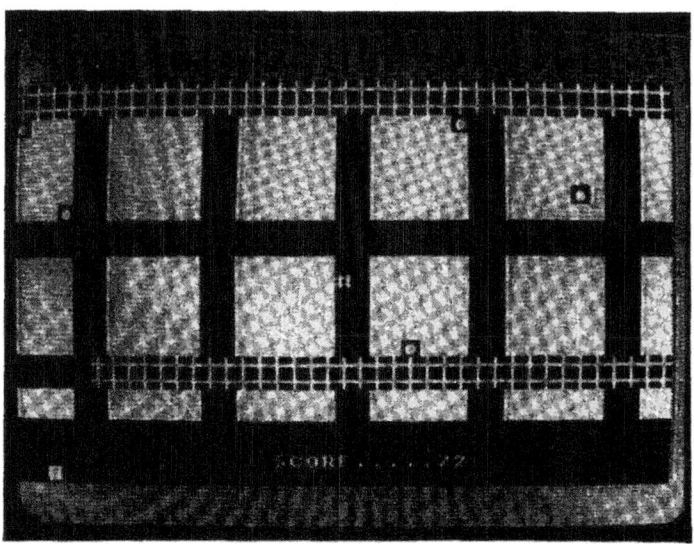

CLASSIFICATION: Evasion/Strategy

In this game, you must move around the maze, dodging everything you can. You must find the compass, which is hidden somewhere within the walls of the ratmaze. You must carefully travel through moving fences, dodge the flying balls and the mines that they lay. You must also avoid the deadly walls or else you will be destroyed. To move through the maze use the keys:

Q=UP
Z=DOWN
I=LEFT
P=RIGHT

any other key stops you from moving

PROGRAMMING SUGGESTIONS

Increase the number of objects you must find to complete the game. Make the objects which are flying round the screen more intelligent and more deadly.

Program Variables

A, I	Dummy variables
O	Character under your program
P	Your position in the maze
SCORE	Your score for the game

Program Structure

```
   3 -   95 Initialize the system
 100 -  150 Call machine program
1000 - 1100 Restart game
2000 - 2040 Give bonus points
```

Listing

> Initialize the system

```
3   GRAPHICS 18:? #6:? #6:? #6:? #6:? #6:? #6:"                    WAIT!!
    !!"
9   POKE 203,4:POKE 204,80:POKE 205,64:POKE 206,156:POKE 16
    96,0:POKE 1697,80
10  FOR T=20000 TO 20479:READ A:POKE T,A:NEXT T
11  DATA 104,165,245,72,165,246,72,169,164,133,245,169,6,13
    3,246,169,0,133,208,169,80
12  DATA 133,209,106,0,162,8,169,0,133,208,169,83,145,208,2
    30,208,208,248,177,245,41
13  DATA 127,24,105,8,16,2,169,8,133,208,169,8,133,207,169
    0,145,208,198,208,198
14  DATA 207,208,246,165,208,24,105,125,133,208,169,8,133,2
    07,169,0,145,208,230,208,198
15  DATA 207,208,246,77,245,230,245,24,113,245,198,245,145,
    245,230,245,230,245,165,209,24
16  DATA 105,8,133,209,202,208,171,104,133,246,104,133,245,
    96
20  DATA 104,160,0,169,0,133,206,169,80,133,209,169,0,145,2
    08,230,208,145,208,165,208,24,105,7
21  DATA 133,208,208,239,165,209,24,105,1,133,209,201,144,2
    08,228,169,0,133,208,169,80,133,209
22  DATA 169,0,145,208,230,208,208,248,24,169,4,101,209,133
    ,209,201,144,208,237,96
23  DATA 104,169,245,72,165,246,72,169,0,133,206,165,6,133,
    209,162,32,160,0,177
24  DATA 208,133,245,160,1,177,208,133,246,160,2,177,205,16,
    0,0,145,245,160,3,177
25  DATA 208,24,101,245,133,245,160,0,145,208,169,0,101,246
    ,201,143,208,2,169,80
26  DATA 133,246,160,1,145,208,160,0,177,245,160,2,145,208,
    160,4,177,208,160,0
27  DATA 145,245,169,5,24,101,208,133,208,202,208,181,104,1
    33,246,104,133,245,96
28  DATA 104,169,0,133,245,169,80,133,246,162,64
29  DATA 160,0,169,128,145,245,200,208,249,230,246
30  DATA 202,208,242,96
31  DATA 104,173,242,2,201,47,240,13,201,23,240,36,201,13,2
    40,59,201,10,240,66,96,165,203,201,128,176,7,165,204
32  DATA 201,81,176,1,96,56,165,203,233,128,133,203,165,204
    ,233,0,133,204,96,165,203,201,128,144,7,165,204,201,131
33  DATA 208,1,96,24,165,203,105,128,133,203,165,204,105,0,
    133,204,96,165,203,41,127,201,0,240,2,198,203,96
34  DATA 165,203,41,127,201,88,176,2,230,203,96
35  DATA 104,165,203,72,165,204,72,165,205,72,165,206,72
36  DATA 169,20,133,207,162,40,160,0,177,203,145,205,200,20
    2,208,248,24,165,203,105,128,133,203,165,204
37  DATA 105,0,133,204,24,165,205,105,40,133,205,165,206,10
    5,0,133,206,198,207,208,214
38  DATA 104,133,206,104,133,205,104,133,204,104,133,203,96
```

```
40    A=USR(20285):A=USR(20119)
50    FOR T=1700 TO 1715 STEP 2:POKE T,64:A=INT(RND(1)*5)+1:I
      F A<4 THEN POKE T+1,256-A:NEXT T:GOTO 60
53    POKE T+1,A-3:NEXT T
60    FOR T=1536 TO 1695 STEP 5:POKE T,INT(RND(1)*100)+14:POK
      E T+1,INT(RND(1)*40)+96
65    POKE T+2,PEEK(PEEK(T)+PEEK(T+1)*256)
70    A=INT(RND(1)*5):IF INT(RND(1)*6)=1 THEN POKE T+3,1:GOTO
       80
75    POKE T+3,125+A
80    POKE T+4,84:NEXT T:SCORE=0
90    GRAPHICS 0:SETCOLOR 2,13,0:SETCOLOR 1,13,7:POSITION 16,
      22:? "SCORE.....":SCORE:SETCOLOR 4,4,4
95    POKE 752,0
```

```
                    Call machine program
```

```
100   A=USR(20186)
103   A=USR(20000)
105   A=USR(20311):P=PEEK(203)+256*PEEK(204)+1428:O=PEEK(P):P
      OKE P,3
110   A=USR(20408)
115   IF O<>0 THEN GOTO 1000
120   POKE P,0
140   POKE 33748,INT(RND(1)*4)+92
145   SCORE=SCORE+1:POSITION 26,22:PRINT SCORE
150   GOTO 100
```

```
                       Restart game
```

```
1000  ? CHR$(125)
1010  IF P=33748 THEN GOTO 2000
1020  GRAPHICS 18:? #6:? #6:? #6:? #6:? #6:"     GAME OVER!"
1030  FOR T=0 TO 400:NEXT T
1040  GRAPHICS 0
1050  POSITION 15,10:? "HIT ANY KEY"
1060  POSITION 15,12:? "FOR ANOTHER"
1070  POSITION 18,14:? "GAME"
1080  POKE 754,0
1090  IF PEEK(754)<>0 THEN RUN
1100  GOTO 1090
```

```
                     Give bonus points
```

```
2000  GRAPHICS 18:? #6:? #6:? #6:? #6:? #6:"     WELL DONE!";
      ? #6:? #6:"   BONUS 1000 PTS.":SCORE=SCORE+1000
2010  POKE 203,4:POKE 204,80
2020  POKE 754,0
2030  IF PEEK(754) THEN GOTO 90
2040  GOTO 2030
```

ChexSum Tables

```
 3 = 2208          33 = 4963         140 = 1095
 9 = 2488          34 = 2032         145 = 1064
10 = 1280          35 = 2479         150 = 112
11 = 3937          36 = 4763        1000 = 343
12 = 3868          37 = 3925        1010 = 577
13 = 3686          38 = 2597        1020 = 2149
14 = 4023          40 = 1186        1030 = 509
15 = 4170          50 = 3697        1040 = 79
16 = 2717          53 = 749         1050 = 1159
20 = 4343          60 = 2987        1060 = 1195
21 = 4352          65 = 1444        1070 = 676
22 = 3765          70 = 2369        1080 = 255
23 = 3623          75 = 600         1090 = 506
24 = 3655          80 = 1014        1100 = 271
25 = 3639          90 = 2643        2000 = 4468
26 = 3544          95 = 253         2010 = 636
27 = 3655         100 = 632         2020 = 255
28 = 2089         103 = 497         2030 = 656
29 = 2183         105 = 2741        2040 = 191
30 = 853          110 = 509
31 = 5147         115 = 362
32 = 5312         120 = 334         TOTAL = 133509
```

2D MAZE

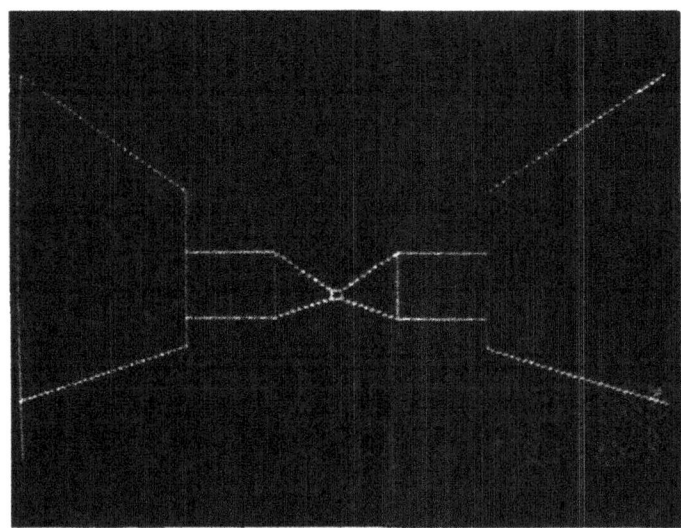

CLASSIFICATION: Skill

You are placed randomly within a maze and must work your way through to the end. The end of the maze is a flashing wall of color. Move forward using the joystick.

PROGRAMMING SUGGESTIONS

Put a time limit on solving the maze. Introduce random teleporters which change your position and orientation; once triggered, they disappear. Increase the size of the maze. Have nasty things chase you! Add secret, invisible passageways that change your position.

Program Variables

```
MZ()        Maze array
J           Current junction
D           Actual junction
MAND$       Machine code for AND instruction
MOR$        Machine code for OR instruction
```

Program Structure

```
 10 - 110   Initialize the game
120 - 140   Scan the keyboard
150 - 180   Move the player
190 - 200   Rotate left or right
210 - 440   Draw the players view
```

Listing

Initialize the game

```
10      GOTO 3000
15      PRINT CHR$(125);"WAIT":DX=9:DY=9:XF=5:YF=9
20      DIM MZ(DX,DY):COLOR 1
30      RESTORE 50
40      FOR I=0 TO DY:FOR J=0 TO DX:READ A:MZ(J,I)=A:NEXT J:NEXT I
50      DATA 15,3,4,7,5,7,5,5,15,5,11,14,5,13,5,13,5,3,10,6,14,11,6,5,5,5,7,11,8,10
60      DATA 10,8,10,6,3,6,11,12,7,9,12,5,9,8,6,12,15,5,13,3,5,5,3,6,15,3,10,2,6,13
70      DATA 7,5,9,10,10,12,9,10,12,5,14,7,5,9,12,5,5,15,5,1,11,14,5,7,7,5,3,10,4,5
80      DATA 11,8,4,9,8,4,9,12,7,5
85      GOTO 110
```

Call MAND and MOR

```
90      LL=USR(ADR(MAND$),(X1*2),15):LL=LL+INT(USR(ADR(MAND$),X1,8)/8):RETURN
100     RR=INT(X1/2)+(USR(ADR(MAND$),X1,1)*8):RETURN
```

Scan the keyboard

```
110     X=INT(RND(0)*6+2):Y=INT(RND(0)*5):D=2^INT(RND(0)*4):GRAPHICS 8:GOSUB 210
120     B=STRIG(1):A=STICK(1):IF A=15 AND B=1 THEN 120
130     IF A=11 THEN X1=D:GOSUB 100:D=RR:GOSUB 210:GOTO 120
140     IF A=7 THEN X1=D:GOSUB 90:D=LL:GOSUB 210:GOTO 120
150     IF USR(ADR(MAND$),D,MZ(X,Y))=1 THEN X=X-1:IF X<0 THEN X=DX
160     IF USR(ADR(MAND$),D,MZ(X,Y))=2 THEN Y=Y+1:IF Y>DY THEN Y=0
170     IF USR(ADR(MAND$),D,MZ(X,Y))=4 THEN X=X+1:IF X>DX THEN X=0
180     IF USR(ADR(MAND$),D,MZ(X,Y))=8 THEN Y=Y-1:IF Y<0 THEN Y=DY
190     GOSUB 210:IF X=XF AND Y=YF THEN GRAPHICS 0:END
200     GOTO 120
```

Draw the players view

```
210   GRAPHICS 8:XN=X:YN=Y:IF USR(ADR(MAND$),D,MZ(X,Y))=0 THE
      N RETURN
220   IF USR(ADR(MAND$),D,MZ(X,Y))=1 THEN XN=X-1:IF XN<0 THEN
       XN=DX
230   IF USR(ADR(MAND$),D,MZ(X,Y))=2 THEN YN=Y+1:IF YN>DY THE
      N YN=0
240   IF USR(ADR(MAND$),D,MZ(X,Y))=4 THEN XN=X+1:IF XN>DX THE
      N XN=0
250   IF USR(ADR(MAND$),D,MZ(X,Y))=8 THEN YN=Y-1:IF YN<0 THEN
       YN=DY
260   PLOT 0,0:DRAWTO 87,57:PLOT 0,159:DRAWTO 87,130:PLOT 319
      ,0:DRAWTO 232,57:PLOT 319,159:DRAWTO 232,130
270   IF USR(ADR(MAND$),MZ(XN,YN),D)=0 THEN 300
280   PLOT 157,103:DRAWTO 162,103:DRAWTO 162,107:DRAWTO 157,1
      07:DRAWTO 157,103
281   PLOT 157,103:DRAWTO 130,85:PLOT 162,103:DRAWTO 189,85
290   PLOT 157,107:DRAWTO 130,116:PLOT 162,107:DRAWTO 189,116
      :GOTO 310
300   PLOT 130,85:DRAWTO 189,85:PLOT 130,116:DRAWTO 189,116
310   X1=D:GOSUB 100:IF USR(ADR(MAND$),MZ(XN,YN),RR)=0 THEN 3
      40
320   PLOT 87,57:DRAWTO 87,130:PLOT 130,85:DRAWTO 87,85:PLOT
      130,116:DRAWTO 87,116
330   IF USR(ADR(MAND$),MZ(XN,YN),D)>0 THEN PLOT 130,85:DRAWT
      O 130,116
340   X1=D:GOSUB 90:IF USR(ADR(MAND$),MZ(XN,YN),LL)=0 THEN 37
      0
350   PLOT 232,57:DRAWTO 232,130:PLOT 189,85:DRAWTO 232,85:PL
      OT 189,116:DRAWTO 232,116
360   IF USR(ADR(MAND$),MZ(XN,YN),D)>0 THEN PLOT 189,85:DRAWT
      O 189,116
370   X1=D:GOSUB 90:IF USR(ADR(MAND$),MZ(XN,YN),LL)>0 THEN 40
      0
380   PLOT 232,57:DRAWTO 189,85:PLOT 232,130:DRAWTO 189,116
390   IF USR(ADR(MAND$),MZ(XN,YN),D)=0 THEN PLOT 189,85:DRAWT
      O 189,116
400   X1=D:GOSUB 100:IF USR(ADR(MAND$),MZ(XN,YN),RR)>0 THEN 4
      30
410   PLOT 87,57:DRAWTO 130,85:PLOT 87,130:DRAWTO 130,116
420   IF USR(ADR(MAND$),MZ(XN,YN),D)=0 THEN PLOT 130,85:DRAWT
      O 130,116
430   IF XN=XF AND YN=YF THEN GRAPHICS 0:PRINT "HOME"
440   RETURN
```

Data for MAND and MOR

```
3000  DATA 104,104,133,213,104,133,212
3010  DATA 104,37,213,133,213,104,37,212,133,212,96
3020  RESTORE 3000:DIM MAND$(18),MOR$(18)
3030  FOR I=1 TO 18:READ A:MAND$(I,I)=CHR$(A):NEXT I
3040  MOR$=MAND$:MOR$(9,9)=CHR$(5):MOR$(14,14)=CHR$(5)
```

```
3050    REM A=USR(ADR(MAND$),X,Y) . A=X AND Y
3060    REM A=USR(ADR(MOR$),X,Y) .A= X OR Y
3070    GOTO 15
```

ChexSum Tables

10 = 159	180 = 2752	360 = 2425
15 = 2234	190 = 1027	370 = 2220
20 = 716	200 = 144	380 = 1809
30 = 215	210 = 2554	390 = 2426
40 = 2293	220 = 2752	400 = 2129
50 = 3539	230 = 2752	410 = 1795
60 = 3539	240 = 2749	420 = 2248
70 = 3539	250 = 2764	430 = 1196
80 = 1187	260 = 3203	440 = 58
85 = 128	270 = 1500	3000 = 1468
90 = 3037	280 = 1968	3010 = 2117
100 = 1869	281 = 1785	3020 = 972
110 = 3113	290 = 1788	3030 = 1859
120 = 1874	300 = 1823	3040 = 2233
130 = 1675	310 = 2145	3070 = 131
140 = 1804	320 = 2905	
150 = 2740	330 = 2247	
160 = 2740	340 = 2332	TOTAL = 106190
170 = 2737	350 = 2755	

MINOTAUR

CLASSIFICATION: Arcade

The objective of this game is to guess a number in the range of 0 to 99. You do it by moving a piece around a board of numbers. As you pass over a number, it is removed from the board and added to your score. If you pass over an X, a clue appears at the top of the board for a short time. If you pass over a question mark, a random number is added to your score. If you pass over a number greater than six as you move around the board, you are pursed by a minotaur. If he captures you, you're dead. Remember, once you pass over a number it is removed from the board and you cannot pass over spaces. If you become encircled by spaces press the fire button to escape. When you have guessed the number, move your piece to the white cursor.

PROGRAMMING SUGGESTIONS

Add different pieces to the board, such as bombs and mines. Place tempory barriers in the path of both the player and the minotaur.

Program Variables

SC	Screen memory
H$	Characters on the screen
R	Row co-ordinate of player's piece
C	Column co-ordinate of player's piece
PO	Player's piece position
PE	Player's piece's previous position
BE	Start of matrix on screen
C1	Column position of minotaur
R1	Row position of minotaur
MA	Minotaur's screen position

Program Structure

```
 10 -   90 Initialize the game and variables
100 -  400 Draw the screen and generate clues
400 -  550 Main loop
560 -  750 Move your player round the screen
850 -  910 Move the minotaur
920 - 1070 Print messagesy
```

Listing

```
10    REM MICRO MINOTAUR
20    CLR
21    DIM RR$(24),CC$(40),CL$(201),H$(11),NU$(2);A$(5),WA$(40
      ),VT$(5)
23    POKE 82,0:PRINT CHR$(125);
24    SP=0:REM SET SPACE CHARACTER
25    IN=128:REM SET INVERSE SPACE
26    MI=13:REM SET THE MINOTAUR CHARACTER
27    XX=56:REM SET CLUE CHARACTER TO X
30    PRINT CHR$(125);
40    SC=40000:CO=40960:C=0:R=0:PO=SC+(R*40)+C:BE=SC+130
60    FOR I=1 TO 24:RR$(I,I)="+":NEXT I
70    FOR I=1 TO 40:CC$(I,I)="→":NEXT I
80    FOR I=1 TO 200:CL$(I,I)=" ":NEXT I
81    FOR I=1 TO 34:WA$(I,I)=" ":NEXT I
90    J=1:FOR I=17 TO 25:H$(J,J)=CHR$(I):J=J+1:NEXT I:H$(10,1
      0)=CHR$(31):H$(11,11)=CHR$(56)
100   FOR I=SC TO SC+39:POKE I,IN:NEXT I
110   FOR I=SC+(23*40)+1 TO SC+(23*40)+38:POKE I,IN:NEXT I
120   FOR I=SC+40 TO SC+(23*39) STEP 40:POKE I,IN:NEXT I
130   FOR I=SC+39 TO SC+(23*40)+39 STEP 40:POKE I,IN:NEXT I
140   POSITION 0,0:PRINT "               MICRO MINOTAUR";"
      PLAYER           ";
150   FOR I=SC+130 TO SC+850 STEP 80
160   FOR J=I TO I+18 STEP 2
170   Q=INT(RND(1)*12):IF Q=0 THEN 170
180   A=ASC(H$(Q,Q))
190   POKE J,A:NEXT J:NEXT I
200   NU=INT(RND(1)*100):IF NU=0 THEN 200
210   NU$=STR$(NU):RA=INT(RND(1)*3):IF RA=0 THEN GOTO 210
220   IF NU<10 THEN NU$(2,2)=NU$(1,1):NU$(1,1)="0"
230   IF RA=1 THEN CL$(1,19)="FIRST DIGIT EQUALS ":CL$(20,20)
      =NU$(2,2)
240   IF RA=2 THEN CL$(1,19)="SECOND DIGIT EQUAL ":CL$(20,20)
      =NU$(1,1)
250   CN=1:FOR I=2 TO NU-1
260   A=NU/I:B=INT(A):IF A<>B THEN 290
270   IF CN=7 THEN 300
280   CL$(((CN*20)+1),(CN*20)+17)="FACTOR OF NUMBER ":CL$(((CN
      *20)+19,(CN*20)+20)=STR$(A):CN=CN+1
290   NEXT I
300   IF NU/2=INT(NU/2) THEN CL$(((CN*20)+1),(CN*20)+18)="THE
       NUMBER IS EVEN"
310   IF NU/2<>INT(NU/2) THEN CL$(((CN*20)+1),(CN*20)+17)="TH
      E NUMBER IS ODD"
320   GB=VAL(NU$(1,1)):FOR I=2 TO 9:A=GB/I:IF A=INT(GB/I) THE
      N GOSUB 1060:GOTO 340
330   NEXT I
340   GB=VAL(NU$(2,2)):FOR I=2 TO 9:A=GB/I:IF A=INT(GB/I) THE
      N GOSUB 1070:GOTO 360
350   NEXT I
360   SD=VAL(NU$(2,2)):IF SD/2=INT(SD/2) THEN CL$((7*20)+1,(7
      *20)+19)="FIRST DIGIT IS EVEN"
370   IF SD/2<>INT(SD/2) THEN CL$((8*20)+1,(8*20)+18)="FIRST
      DIGIT IS ODD"
```

```
380     SD=VAL(NU$(2,2)):IF SD/2=INT(SD/2) THEN CL$((8*20)+1,(8
        *20)+20)="SECOND DIGIT IS EVEN"
390     IF SD/2<>INT(SD/2) THEN CL$((8*20)+1,(8*20)+19)="SECOND
         DIGIT IS ODD"
400     FOR I=1 TO 9:IF I*I=NU THEN CL$((20*9)+1,(20*9)+19)="PR
        ODUCT OF A SQUARE"
410     NEXT I
420     HO=BE+10:POKE HO,IN
430     C1=6:R1=6:MA=BE+(R1*40)+C1:VE=PEEK(MA):POKE MA,MI
440     C=10:R=18:PO=BE+(R*40)+C:VA=PEEK(PO):POKE PO,209
450     B=STRIG(1):A=STICK(1):IF A=15 AND B=1 THEN 550
460     IF A=14 THEN GOSUB 560
470     IF A=13 THEN GOSUB 620
480     IF A=11 THEN GOSUB 680
490     IF A=7 THEN GOSUB 740
500     IF B=0 THEN GOTO 1040
510     GOSUB 850
520     POSITION 0,0:PRINT "↓↓→→";WA$
530     TT=TT+CU
540     POSITION 0,0:PRINT RR$(1,22);CC$(1,7);"LAST SCORE:";
        CU;"  TOTAL SCORE:";TT
550     CU=0:POKE MA,141:GOTO 450
560     IF R=0 THEN RETURN
570     R=R-2:PE=PO:PO=BE+(R*40)+C:DA=PEEK(PO):IF DA=SP THEN R=
        R+2:PO=BE+(R*40)+C:RETURN
580     IF DA=MI THEN GOTO 920
590     GOSUB 800
600     POKE PE,VA:FL=PEEK(PE):CU=FL-16:POKE PE,SP:VA=PEEK(PO)
610     POKE PO,209:RETURN
620     IF R=18 THEN RETURN
630     R=R+2:PE=PO:PO=BE+(R*40)+C:DA=PEEK(PO):IF DA=SP THEN R=
        R-2:PO=BE+(R*40)+C:RETURN
640     IF DA=MI THEN GOTO 920
650     GOSUB 800
660     POKE PE,VA:FL=PEEK(PE):CU=FL-16:POKE PE,SP
670     VA=PEEK(PO):POKE PO,209:RETURN
680     IF C=0 THEN RETURN
690     C=C-2:PE=PO:PO=BE+(R*40)+C:DA=PEEK(PO):IF DA=SP THEN C=
        C+2:PO=BE+(R*40)+C:RETURN
700     IF DA=MI THEN GOTO 920
710     GOSUB 800
720     POKE PE,VA:FL=PEEK(PE):CU=FL-16:POKE PE,SP
730     VA=PEEK(PO):POKE PO,209:RETURN
740     IF C=18 THEN RETURN
750     C=C+2:PE=PO:PO=BE+(R*40)+C:DA=PEEK(PO):IF DA=SP THEN C=
        C-2:PO=BE+(R*40)+C:RETURN
760     IF DA=MI THEN GOTO 920
770     GOSUB 800
780     POKE PE,VA:FL=PEEK(PE):CU=FL-16:POKE PE,SP
790     VA=PEEK(PO):POKE PO,209:RETURN
800     IF DA=63 THEN CU=INT(RND(1)*10)
810     FU=INT(RND(9)*10)
820     DI=(FU*20)+1:IF DA=XX THEN POSITION 0,0:PRINT CC$(1,5);
        RR$(1,2);CL$(DI,DI+19);:GOSUB 1050
830     IF DA=IN THEN GOSUB 1000
840     RETURN
850     IF CU<6 THEN RETURN
860     IF C1>C THEN C1=C1-2
```

```
870   IF C1<C THEN C1=C1+2
880   IF R1>R THEN R1=R1-2
890   IF R1<R THEN R1=R1+2
900   POKE MA,VE:MA=BE+(R1*40)+C1:IF PEEK(MA)=209 THEN GOSUB
      920:STOP
910   VE=PEEK(MA):POKE MA,MI:RETURN
920   PRINT CHR$(125);:PRINT RR$(1,10);"THE MINOTAUR HAS EATE
      N YOU"
930   POSITION 0,0:PRINT RR$(1,13);"THE NUMBER WAS ";NU
940   PRINT :PRINT :PRINT
950   PRINT "DO YOU WANT ANOTHER GAME(Y/N):";
960   INPUT A$:IF A$="" THEN PRINT "↑";:GOTO 960
970   IF A$="Y" THEN GOTO 20
980   IF A$="N" THEN END
990   GOTO 960
1000  PRINT CHR$(125):PRINT RR$(1,2);CC$(1,3);"WHAT IS THE NU
      MBER";:INPUT VT$
1005  VT=VAL(VT$)
1010  IF VT<>NU THEN PRINT "WRONG THE NUMBER WAS ";NU:GOTO 94
      0
1020  PRINT "CONGRATULATIONS YOU HAVE BEATEN MINOTAUR"
1030  GOTO 940
1040  PRINT CHR$(125);:GOTO 930
1050  FOR I=1 TO 300:NEXT I:RETURN
1060  CL$((6*20)+1,(6*20)+19)="FACTOR SECOND DIGIT":CL$((6*20
      )+20,(6*20)+20)=STR$(I):RETURN
1070  CL$((5*20)+1,(5*20)+18)="FACTOR FIRST DIGIT":CL$((5*20)
      +20,(5*20)+20)=STR$(I):RETURN
```

ChexSum Tables

```
 20 =   40          350 = 177          740 =  388
 21 = 2865          360 = 4529         750 = 4994
 23 =  682          370 = 3465         760 =  542
 24 = 1778          380 = 4592         770 =  121
 25 = 1770          390 = 3520         780 = 2060
 26 = 2386          400 = 3758         790 = 1008
 27 = 2183          410 =  177         800 = 1300
 30 =  356          420 =  938         810 =  861
 40 = 3214          430 = 2968         820 = 3579
 60 = 1434          440 = 2850         830 =  518
 70 = 1465          450 = 1974         840 =   58
 80 = 1406          460 =  554         850 =  389
 81 = 1459          470 =  490         860 =  942
 90 = 4786          480 =  584         870 =  940
100 = 1279          490 =  511         880 =  946
110 = 2312          500 =  451         890 =  944
120 = 1914          510 =  201         900 = 2350
130 = 2102          520 =  491         910 = 1073
140 = 7439          530 =  645         920 = 2811
150 = 1127          540 = 6320         930 = 1925
160 =  784          550 =  928         940 =  179
170 = 1327          560 =  301         950 = 2126
180 = 1022          570 = 4998         960 =  788
190 =  748          580 =  542         970 =  487
200 = 1204          590 =  121         980 =  370
210 = 1897          600 = 2703         990 =  216
220 = 2100          610 =  379        1000 = 2936
230 = 3477          620 =  389        1005 =  592
240 = 3445          630 = 4998        1010 = 2352
250 =  980          640 =  542        1020 = 2985
260 = 1873          650 =  121        1030 =  184
270 =  409          660 = 2060        1040 =  549
280 = 5274          670 = 1008        1050 =  695
290 =  177          680 =  300        1060 = 4652
300 = 3676          690 = 4994        1070 = 4592
310 = 3582          700 =  542
320 = 3386          710 =  121        TOTAL = 199733
330 =  177          720 = 2060
340 = 3436          730 = 1008
```

BATTLESHIP

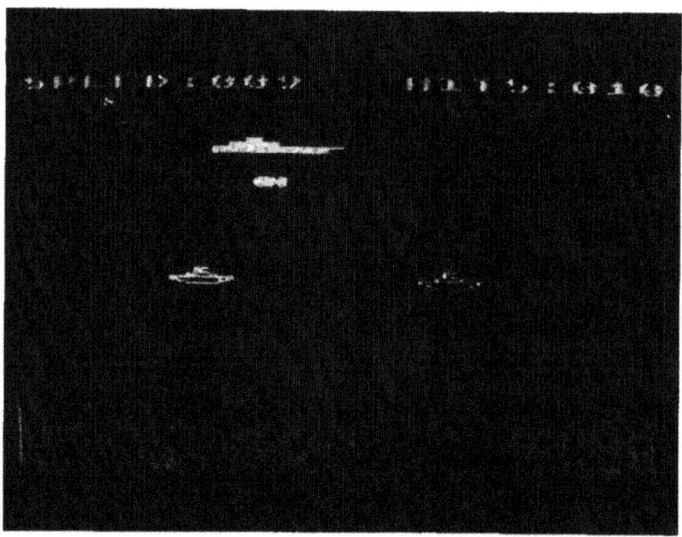

CLASSIFICATION: Arcade

You are the commander of a battleship and must destroy enemy submarines. You destroy them by dropping depth charges on them. Each time one of them escapes the escape counter is incremented. Each time you hit one, the hit counter is incremented.

PROGRAMMING SUGGESTIONS

Add different kinds of submarines to your fleet of enemies and give them varying degrees of strength. Fit the submarines with different kinds of weapons, for example some sea to air missiles. Use the joystick to move your battleship left and right and press the fire button to launch a depth charge.

Program
Variables

I	General purpose variable
X2	X position of battleship
Y2	Y Position of battleship
X1	X position of submarine 1
Y1	Y position of submarine 1
X3	X position of submarine 2
Y3	Y position of submarine 2
X4	X position of depth charge
Y4	Y position of depth charge

Program
Structure

2 -	85	Clear out memory and read in data
100 -	130	Data for players
200 -	350	Set up players
1000 -	1041	Main loop
2000 -	2999	Initialize game
3000 -	3599	Move the battleship
4000 -	4999	Move the submarines
5000 -	5999	Move the mine
6000 -	6999	Update the score
7000 -	7030	Check for collision
9000 -	9090	Data for machine language program

Listing

```
2       CLR
6       FOR I=30720 TO 30798:READ A:POKE I,A:NEXT I
7       FOR I=33792 TO 33792+1023:POKE I,0:NEXT I
9       FOR I=28672 TO 29050:READ A:POKE I,A:NEXT I
10      POKE 106,128
20      PM=PEEK(106):PMBASE=PM*256
30      GRAPHICS 1
40      POKE 559,62
50      POKE 53277,3
60      POKE 54279,PM
70      POKE 53256,2
80      POKE 704,87:POKE 705,77:POKE 706,77
85      POKE 707,77
100     DATA 24,16,24,36,255,129,66,60,0,0,0,0,0,0,0,0,0,0,0,0
110     DATA 0,0,32,32,112,112,255,254,254,0,0,0,0,0,0,0,0,0,0,0
120     DATA 24,16,24,36,255,129,66,60,0,0,0,0,0,0,0,0,0,0,0,0
130     DATA 0,0,123,255,255,123,0,0,0,0,0,0,0,0,0,0,0,0
200     POKE 53256,1
210     POKE 53257,3
220     POKE 53258,1
230     POKE 53259,2
300     POKE 704,125
310     POKE 705,31
320     POKE 706,118
340     POKE 707,175
350     A=USR(28672,X1,Y1,X2,Y2,X3,Y3,X4,Y4)
1000    GOSUB 2000
1010    GOSUB 3000:REM BATTLESHIP
1020    GOSUB 4000:REM SUBMARINES
1025    GOSUB 5000:REM CHARGE
1027    GOSUB 6000:REM UPDATE
1030    A=USR(28672,X1,Y1,X2,Y2,X3,Y3,X4,Y4)
1040    GOSUB 7000:REM CHECK
1041    GOTO 1010
2000    POSITION 0,0
2020    X2=100:Y2=28:Y4=220:POKE 53278,0
2025    GOSUB 4500:Y1=Y:GOSUB 4500:Y3=Y
2999    RETURN
3000    REM BATTLESHIP
3005    A=STICK(1):POKE 53278,0
3010    IF A=11 THEN GOSUB 3100:RETURN
3020    IF A=7 THEN GOSUB 3200:RETURN
3030    IF STRIG(1)=0 THEN GOSUB 3500:RETURN
3040    RETURN
3100    REM LEFT
3110    IF X2=0 THEN RETURN
3120    X2=X2-4:RETURN
3200    REM RIGHT
3210    IF X2=128 THEN RETURN
3220    X2=X2+4:RETURN
3500    REM DROP DEPTH CHARGE
3501    IF IN THEN RETURN
3505    X4=X2:Y4=Y2+8:IN=1
3599    RETURN
4000    REM SUBMARINES
```

```
4005    GOSUB 4100:GOSUB 4200:RETURN
4100    REM MOVE SUBMARINE 1
4105    IF X1>180 THEN GOSUB 4500:ES=ES+1:Y1=Y:X1=0:RETURN
4110    X1=X1+(RND(1)*4):RETURN
4199    RETURN
4200    REM MOVE SUBMARINE 2
4205    IF X3>180 THEN GOSUB 4500:ES=ES+1:Y3=Y:X3=0:RETURN
4210    X3=X3+(RND(1)*4):RETURN
4299    RETURN
4500    Y=RND(9)*150:IF Y>150 THEN 4500
4505    IF Y<60 THEN 4500
4510    RETURN
4999    RETURN
5000    REM
5005    IF IN=0 THEN RETURN
5010    IF Y4>150 THEN Y4=220:IN=0:RETURN
5015    Y4=Y4+4:RETURN
5999    RETURN
6000    REM
6005    POSITION 0,0:PRINT #6;"ESCAPED:";ES;" HITS:";HI;"  ";
6999    RETURN
7000    REM
7005    A=PEEK(53263):IF A=0 THEN RETURN
7010    IF A=1 THEN GOSUB 7100:RETURN
7015    IF A=4 THEN GOSUB 7200:RETURN
7020    IF A=5 THEN GOSUB 7100:GOSUB 7200:RETURN
7030    RETURN
7100    HI=HI+1:X1=0:GOSUB 4500:Y1=Y:IN=0:POKE 53278,0:Y4=220:R
        ETURN
7200    HI=HI+1:X3=0:GOSUB 4500:Y3=Y:IN=0:POKE 53278,0:Y4=220:R
        ETURN
7999    RETURN
9000    DATA 104,104,104,141,61,113,104,104,141,60,113,104,104,
        141,75,113,104,104,141,74
9005    DATA 113,104,104,141,89,113,104,104,141,88,113,104,104,
        141,103,113,104,104,141,102
9010    DATA 113,32,45,112,96,120,32,8,113,160,14,162,0,189,53,
        113,149,176,232,136
9015    DATA 208,247,32,170,112,160,14,162,0,181,176,157,53,113
        ,232,136,208,247,160,14
9020    DATA 162,0,189,67,113,149,176,232,136,208,247,32,170,11
        2,160,14,162,0,181,176
9025    DATA 157,67,113,232,136,208,247,160,14,162,0,189,81,113
        ,149,176,232,136,208,247
9030    DATA 32,170,112,160,14,162,0,181,176,157,81,113,232,136
        ,208,247,160,14,162,0
9035    DATA 189,95,113,149,176,232,136,208,247,32,170,112,160,
        14,162,0,181,176,157,95
9040    DATA 113,232,136,208,247,32,22,113,88,96,165,183,197,18
        2,240,68,160,0,165,184
9045    DATA 24,105,46,145,176,169,32,24,101,182,168,166,185,16
        9,0,145,178,200,202,16
9050    DATA 250,169,32,24,101,183,141,116,113,162,0,142,109,11
        3,166,185,172,109,113,177
9055    DATA 180,238,109,113,172,116,113,145,178,238,116,113,20
        2,16,237,165,183,133,182,165
9060    DATA 184,133,189,96,165,184,197,189,208,182,96,173,112,
        113,41,15,170,189,36,113
```

```
9065  DATA 238,112,113,96,160,14,162,0,181,176,157,117,113,23
      2,136,208,247,96,160,14
9070  DATA 162,0,189,117,113,149,176,232,136,208,247,96,1,2,3
      ,4,5,10,7,8
9075  DATA 7,8,11,4,2,4,1,4,8,0,208,0,132,0,120,0,0,0,8,0
9080  DATA 16,0,0,1,208,0,133,20,120,0,0,0,8,0,16,0,0,2,208,0

9085  DATA 134,40,120,0,0,0,8,0,16,0,0,3,208,0,135,60,120,0,0
      ,0
9090  DATA 8,0,0,0,0,0,0,79,0,0,0,0,0,0,0,0,141,30,208
```

ChexSum Tables

2 = 40	1040 = 749	5999 = 58
6 = 1359	1041 = 143	6005 = 1864
7 = 1421	2000 = 113	6999 = 58
9 = 1631	2020 = 1575	7005 = 990
10 = 277	2025 = 1247	7010 = 613
20 = 1121	2999 = 58	7015 = 617
30 = 144	3005 = 889	7020 = 887
40 = 420	3010 = 565	7030 = 58
50 = 406	3020 = 556	7100 = 2894
60 = 472	3030 = 640	7200 = 2902
70 = 372	3040 = 58	7999 = 58
80 = 1185	3110 = 304	9000 = 3800
85 = 361	3120 = 609	9005 = 3900
100 = 2502	3210 = 410	9010 = 3548
110 = 2580	3220 = 608	9015 = 3747
120 = 2502	3501 = 257	9020 = 3711
130 = 2280	3505 = 1368	9025 = 3824
200 = 371	3599 = 58	9030 = 3638
210 = 374	4005 = 460	9035 = 3778
220 = 373	4105 = 2106	9040 = 3730
230 = 375	4110 = 993	9045 = 3719
300 = 278	4199 = 58	9050 = 3845
310 = 289	4205 = 2118	9055 = 4013
320 = 267	4210 = 1001	9060 = 3852
340 = 361	4299 = 58	9065 = 3760
350 = 2407	4500 = 1289	9070 = 3163
1000 = 145	4505 = 545	9075 = 2355
1010 = 1092	4510 = 58	9080 = 2537
1020 = 1117	4999 = 58	9085 = 2637
1025 = 794	5005 = 313	9090 = 2191
1027 = 835	5010 = 1215	
1030 = 2407	5015 = 618	
		TOTAL = 128402

CRYPT

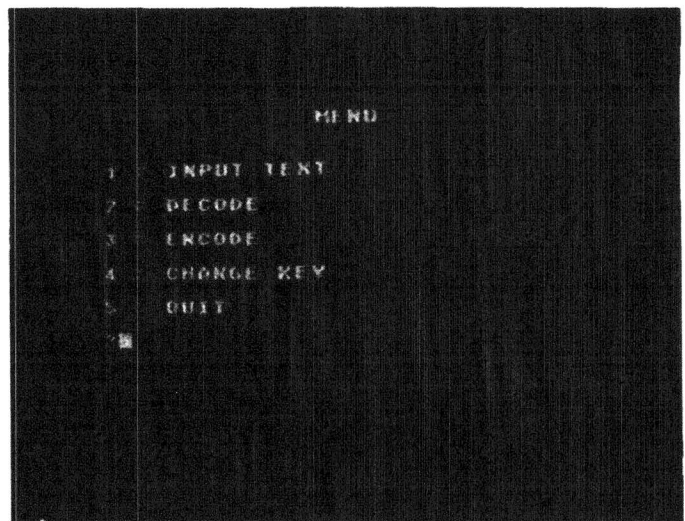

CLASSIFICATION: Passive

This program has a very good software random number generator. This is used instead of the normal rnd(0) function because the sequence of numbers generated by this method is repeatable. Changing the seed numbers, which should be prime, will change the numbers produced by the random routine which, in turn, alters the results of the encode and decode routines. The program is self prompting and the only thing to remember is that the seed numbers should be prime.

PROGRAMMING SUGGESTIONS

It should be possible to make this program work on text files from tape or disk and to work on larger amounts of text.

Program Variables

C	Used in random routine
CODE$	Holds result of encode or decode
FLAG	Flag
H$	List of allowable text characters
KEYA	User key A
KEYB	User key B
LOOP	Loop counter
MAIN$	Holds text
Q	Local
SEEDA	Seed A for random routine
SEEDB	Seed B for random routine
T$	Local string
TEST	Flag for print routine
Y	Local
Z	Local

Program Structure

10		Jump to initialization routine
11		Error message
12		Error Message
20	- 27	Input and check text
30	- 32	Input new keys
100	- 160	Main loop
900		Set for decode
1000		Set for encode
1005	- 3020	Encode or decode
4000	- 4050	Random number generator
5000		Delay loop
20000	- 21000	Initialization routine
30000	- 30040	The modulo arithmetic routine
31000		The good bye routine

Listing

```
10   GOTO 20000
11   ? :? "1.TO.5.ONLY":GOSUB 5000:GOTO 100
12   ? :? :? "INVALID.CHARACTER":GOSUB 5000:GOTO 20
```

```
Jump to initialization routine
```

```
20   FLAG=0:? CHR$(125):? "UPPER.CASE.ALPHA.AND.NUMBERS
     .ONLY ":POSITION 2,4:INPUT MAIN$
21   FOR X=1 TO LEN(MAIN$):X$=MAIN$(X,X)
22   IF X$=" ." THEN GOTO 26
23   IF X$>="0" AND X$<="9" THEN GOTO 26
24   IF X$>="A" AND X$<="Z" THEN GOTO 26
25   FLAG=1
26   NEXT X:IF FLAG THEN GOTO 12
27   GOTO 100
```

```
Input and check text
```

```
30   ? CHR$(125):? "NOTE.NUMBERS.SHOULD.BE.PRIME":? :? :?
31   ? "KEY.A.=";KEYA;" ...KEY.B=";KEYB:? :? "NEW.VALUE.FOR
     KEY.A";:INPUT KEYA
32   ? :? "NEW.VALUE.FOR.KEY.B";:INPUT KEYB
100  ? CHR$(125)
110  POSITION 15,0:? "MENU"
120  ? :? :? "1.=.INPUT.TEXT":? :? "2.=.DECODE":? :? "3.=.
     ENCODE":? :? "4.=.CHANGE.KEY":? :? "5.=.QUIT"
130  ? :INPUT X$:IF LEN(X$)=0 THEN 100
140  T$=X$(1,1):IF T$<"1" OR T$>"5" THEN GOTO 11
150  X=VAL(X$):IF X<1 OR X>5 THEN 11
160  ON X GOTO 20,900,1000,30,31000
```

```
Set for decode
```

```
900  TEST=0:? CHR$(125):? :? :? "WAIT.DECODING":? :? :? :GOT
     O 1005
```

```
1000    TEST=1:? CHR$(125):? :? :? "WAIT ENCODING":? :? :?
1005    IF LEN(MAIN$)=0 THEN ? "NO TEXT":GOSUB 5000:GOTO 100
1010    SEEDA=KEYA:SEEDB=KEYB:CODE$=""
1020    FOR LOOP=1 TO LEN(MAIN$)
1030    T$=MAIN$(LOOP,LOOP)
1040    FOR X=1 TO 37:IF T$=H$(X,X) THEN Q=X
1050    NEXT X
1060    GOSUB 4000:X=C:Y=37:GOSUB 30000
1070    IF  NOT TEST THEN Q=Q-Z:IF Q<1 THEN Q=Q+37
1080    IF TEST THEN Q=Q+Z:IF Q>37 THEN Q=Q-37
1090    CODE$(LOOP,LOOP)=H$(Q,Q)
1100    NEXT LOOP:? CHR$(125)
1110    IF TEST THEN ? :? :? "CYPHER IS:":GOSUB 3000
1120    IF  NOT TEST THEN ? :? :? "PLAINTEXT IS:":GOSUB 3000
1130    ? :? "PRESS ENTER";:INPUT T$
1140    GOTO 100
3000    ? :? :? CHR$(34);CODE$;CHR$(34):MAIN$=CODE$
3010    ? :? :? "IGNORE ";CHR$(34)
3020    ? :RETURN
```

Random number generator

```
4000    C=SEEDA+SEEDB
4010    IF C>32767 THEN C=C-32768
4020    C=C*2
4030    IF C>32767 THEN C=C-32767
4040    SEEDA=SEEDB:SEEDB=C
4050    RETURN :REM ■C=RND■
```

Delay loop

```
5000    FOR X=1 TO 500:NEXT X:RETURN
```

```
20000 KEYA=7:KEYB=32633:REM **PRIME**
20001 SEEDA=KEYA:SEEDB=KEYB
20010 DIM MAIN$(255),CODE$(255)
20020 MAIN$="":CODE$=""
20030 DIM H$(37)
20040 H$="0123456789.ABCDEFGHIJKLMNOPQRSTUVWXYZ"
20050 SETCOLOR 4,0,0:SETCOLOR 1,0,15:SETCOLOR 2,0,0
20060 DIM X$(9),T$(9)
21000 GOTO 100
```

> The modulo arithmetic routine

```
30000 Z=X/Y
30010 Z=Z-INT(Z)
30020 Z=Z+1/(Y*10)
30030 Z=INT(Z*Y)
30040 RETURN
```

> The good bye routine

```
31000 ? :? :? :? "SO LONG":END
```

ChexSum Tables

10 = 114	1000 = 2307	4030 = 1131
11 = 1228	1005 = 1398	4040 = 667
12 = 1881	1010 = 1038	4050 = 1543
20 = 3645	1020 = 615	5000 = 665
21 = 1436	1030 = 822	20000 = 2320
22 = 434	1040 = 1685	20001 = 793
23 = 746	1050 = 161	20010 = 865
24 = 796	1060 = 1169	20020 = 556
25 = 328	1070 = 1737	20030 = 418
26 = 481	1080 = 1749	20040 = 2886
27 = 112	1090 = 1278	20050 = 860
30 = 2797	1100 = 531	20060 = 705
31 = 3104	1110 = 1329	21000 = 112
32 = 1671	1120 = 1620	30000 = 577
100 = 343	1130 = 1186	30010 = 773
110 = 616	1140 = 112	30020 = 924
120 = 4361	3000 = 1422	30030 = 770
130 = 739	3010 = 1044	30040 = 58
140 = 1497	3020 = 127	31000 = 875
150 = 1268	4000 = 573	
160 = 795	4010 = 1132	
900 = 2433	4020 = 521	TOTAL = 72569

DUNGEONS

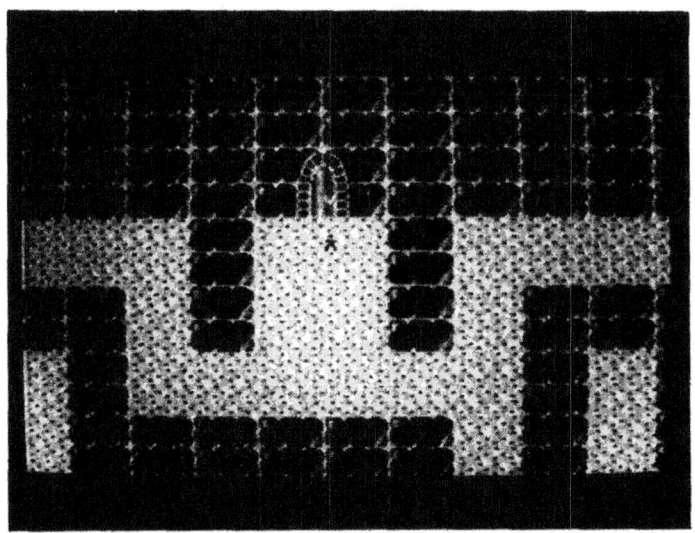

CLASSIFICATION: Logic

Move your man round the maze of dungeons trying to find the exit. There are three dungeons and each one has an exit. Hitting the walls causes you to go back to the start of the maze. When you find an exit, move into it to reach the next level.

PROGRAMMING SUGGESTIONS

Increase the number of mazes in the game. Put objects in the maze which can eat you or send you back to the start.

Program Variables

LEVEL   Level you are playing.
MAXLEVELS   Maximium number of levels
T,A,A$,K,N   Dummy variables
COV   Counter for footsteps

Program Structure

      1 -   80   Intialization
    100 -   150   Main Loop
    400 -   430   Crash into wall
   1000 - 1010   More intialization
  15000 - 15110   Completed maze
  30000 - 30362   Even more initialization

Listing

```
                    ┌─────────────────────────────────────┐
                    │  Intialization                      │
                    └─────────────────────────────────────┘

1       DIM A$(32):? CHR$(125):POSITION 10.16:? "WAIT A MOMENT"
2       GOSUB 10000
3       GRAPHICS 18:? #6:? #6:? #6:? #6:? #6:"▲▲▲▲▲WAIT!!
        !!"
9       POKE 203,41:POKE 204,80:POKE 205,64:POKE 206,156
10      RESTORE 11:FOR T=20246 TO 20479:READ A:POKE T,A:NEXT T
11      DATA 104,162,64,169,0,133,208,169,80,133,209,160,0,169,
        64,145,208
12      DATA 200,169,65,145,208,200,169,66,145,208,200,169,67,1
        45,208,200,192
13      DATA 128,208,232,169,68,145,208,200,169,69,145,208,200,
        169,70,145,208
14      DATA 200,169,71,145,208,200,208,234,230,209,202,208,205
        ,96
31      DATA 104,173,242,2,201,47,240,13,201,23,240,36,201,13,2
        40,59,201,10,240,66,96,165,203,201,128,176,7,165,204
32      DATA 201,81,176,1,96,56,165,203,233,128,133,203,165,204
        ,233,0,133,204,96,165,203,201,128,144,7,165,204,201,131
33      DATA 208,1,96,24,165,203,105,128,133,203,165,204,105,0,
        133,204,96,165,203,41,127,201,0,240,2,198,203,96
34      DATA 165,203,41,127,201,88,176,2,230,203,96
35      DATA 104,165,203,72,165,204,72,165,205,72,165,206,72
36      DATA 169,24,133,207,162,40,160,0,177,203,145,205,200,20
        2,208,248,24,165,203,105,128,133,203,165,204
37      DATA 105,0,133,204,24,165,205,105,40,133,205,165,206,10
        5,0,133,206,198,207,208,214
38      DATA 104,133,206,104,133,205,104,133,204,104,133,203,96
40      LEVEL=1:MAXLEVELS=4
50      GOSUB 1000
60      GRAPHICS 0:POKE 756,144:SETCOLOR 2,12,8:SETCOLOR 1,0,0
80      COU=4
100     A=USR(20311):A=USR(20408):IF PEEK(40379)<>89 THEN GOSUB
        400
105     POKE 40379,88
110     IF PEEK(203)+256*PEEK(204)=33705 THEN GOSUB 15000
120     COU=COU-1:IF NOT COU THEN COU=2:FOR T=0 TO 30 STEP 10:
        SOUND 2,T,0,10:NEXT T:SOUND 2,0,0,0
150     GOTO 100

                    ┌─────────────────────────────────────┐
                    │  Crash into wall                    │
                    └─────────────────────────────────────┘

400     FOR T=0 TO 30 STEP 5:SOUND 1,T,0,10:NEXT T:SOUND 1,0,0,
        0
410     POKE 754,0:POKE 203,41:POKE 204,80
420     FOR T=0 TO 30:POKE 756,224:POKE 756,144:NEXT T
430     RETURN
```

More intialization

```
1000  RESTORE 30000+LEVEL*100:GRAPHICS 20:COLOR 1:A=USR(26246
      )
1010  FOR T=0 TO 31:READ A$
1020  FOR N=1 TO 32
1030  C=20480+T*512+(N-1)*4
1040  IF  NOT (ASC(A$(N))-32) THEN FOR A=0 TO 3:FOR B=0 TO 3:
      POKE C+A*128+B,89:NEXT B:NEXT A:PLOT N+24,T+8
1050  NEXT N:NEXT T
1060  FOR T=0 TO 3:FOR N=0 TO 3:POKE 21050+N+T*128,72+N+T*4:N
      EXT N:NEXT T
1070  FOR T=0 TO 3:FOR N=0 TO 3:POKE 34362+N+T*128,72+N+T*4:N
      EXT N:NEXT T
1100  RETURN
10000 POKE 756,144
10010 FOR T=0 TO 1023:POKE 36864+T,PEEK(57344+T):NEXT T
10020 RESTORE 10100+(INT(RND(1)*2)*21):FOR T=37376 TO 37439:R
      EAD A:POKE T,A:NEXT T:RESTORE 10130
10021 FOR T=37440 TO 37583:READ A:POKE T,A:NEXT T:RETURN
10100 DATA 0,127,213,175,223,175,95,127,0,31,191,255,255,255,
      255,255,0,243,255,255,255,255,255,255
10110 DATA 0,240,252,254,254,254,254,250,255,255,255,255,255,
      255,127,31,255,255,255,255,255,255,247,231
10120 DATA 255,255,255,255,253,250,253,255,244,250,244,234,86
      ,170,84,60
10121 DATA 0,127,85,106,85,106,85,106,0,255,85,170,85,170,85,
      170,0,255,85,170,85,170,85,170
10122 DATA 0,255,87,171,87,171,87,171,85,106,85,106,85,106,12
      7,127,85,170,85,170,85,170,255,255
10123 DATA 85,170,85,170,85,170,255,255,87,171,87,171,87,171,
      255,255
10130 DATA 0,227,255,255,255,255,254,254,0,240,252,231,158,63
      ,222,239,0,7,63,103,249,126,251,119
10135 DATA 0,248,253,255,255,255,127,127
10140 DATA 252,253,251,251,249,246,247,231,244,113,130,229,20
      2,21,202,213,47,78,161,87,171,80,171,83
10150 DATA 63,191,223,223,159,111,239,239,0,143,239,239,240,2
      39,239,239,42,149,170,149,42,149,170,149
10160 DATA 168,85,169,85,184,125,185,17,8,247,247,247,15,247,
      247,247,240,239,239,239,240,239,239,239
10170 DATA 42,149,170,149,42,149,170,149,128,69,169,85,168,85
      ,169,85,15,247,247,247,15,247,247,247
10180 DATA 24,24,0,126,24,60,102,102
10190 DATA 0,24,0,0,3,0,48,0
```

Completed maze

```
15000 FOR T=37376 TO 37567 STEP 8:RESTORE 15100:FOR N=0 TO 3:
      FOR K=0 TO 7:READ A:POKE T+K,A:NEXT K:NEXT N
15010 FOR K=T TO (T+7):POKE K,0:NEXT K:SOUND 0,INT(RND(1)*255
      ),0,10:NEXT T:SOUND 0,0,0,0
```

```
15020 LEVEL=LEVEL+1:IF LEVEL=MAXLEVELS THEN GOTO 15060
15030 GRAPHICS 18:POSITION 0,5:? #6:"▲▲▲▲▲▲LEVEL▲":LEVEL:FOR
      T=0 TO 255:SOUND 0,T,10,10:NEXT T:SOUND 0,0,0,0
15040 GOSUB 10000:POP :POKE 203,41:POKE 204,80:GOTO 50
15060 GRAPHICS 18:POSITION 0,5:? #6:"▲▲▲▲▲▲▲THE▲END."
15070 FOR T=0 TO 1000:NEXT T:GRAPHICS 0:END
15100 DATA 126,255,191,223,159,223,159,126,100,230,175,235,25
      ,94,224,71
15110 DATA 192,134,14,12,0,64,193,99,128,130,4,0,0,64,64,1
20000 FOR T=0 TO 3:FOR N=0 TO 3:POKE 21054+N+T*128,72+N+T*4:N
      EXT N:NEXT T
20100 GOTO 20100
30100 DATA ................................
30102 DATA ................................
30104 DATA  ....    .        .   .       .......
30106 DATA  ....  .  ...      .  ...  .  .....
30108 DATA  ....  .    ..          .  .  .....
30110 DATA  ....  ...      ......       .....
30112 DATA  ....    ...         .      .....
30114 DATA  .....    .    .....  . .  .....
30116 DATA  DATA  ..   . ..        .    . .....
30118 DATA  ....  .     .  ...   . ........  .....
30120 DATA  ....  ....            .       .....
30122 DATA  ....  ...  ..............   ...  .....
30124 DATA  ....       . .      .      .     .....
30126 DATA  DATA    .  .  ....   .       .....
30128 DATA  ....        .  .    .  .  .     .....
30130 DATA  .....   .....   .    .       .....
30132 DATA  ....        .   .  .......  .....
30134 DATA  .....   ........   .  .      .....
30136 DATA  ....     .       ..  .........  .....
30138 DATA  DATA  ....   .. ..   ..      .    .....
30140 DATA  ....       .  .  .......       .....
30142 DATA  ....   .  ..    .          ......
30143 DATA  ....  .   ....     ......   .....
30144 DATA  ....  .   ....     ......   .....
30145 DATA  ....     .  ......    .    .....
30146 DATA  ....  ......       .  .      ......
30148 DATA  ....     .  ...  .       ......
30150 DATA  ....    .  .......  ..      .....
30152 DATA  ....  .              .        .....
30154 DATA ................................
30156 DATA ................................
30158 DATA ................................
30200 DATA ................................
30202 DATA ................................
30204 DATA  ....         .        .       .....
30206 DATA  ....  .      . ...               .....
30208 DATA  ....  .    . .      .  .  .    .....
30210 DATA  ....  .....    ..   ..  ..   .....
30212 DATA  ....        .      ..   .     . .....
30214 DATA  ....  .   ..  ...............  .....
30216 DATA  ....   .  ..               .    .....
```

```
30218 DATA ....  .  . .............  . ..........
30220 DATA ....  .                  . .  .......
30222 DATA ....  .......  .  . ..  ..  .   .....
30224 DATA ....  .  .      .  . ..  ..  ..  -  .....
30226 DATA ....    . ............ .       .  .  .....
30228 DATA .........  .           .  .  .  .  .....
30230 DATA ....       .  ............  .  .  .....
30232 DATA ....  ......  .         -  .  .   .....
30234 DATA ....  .      . .............    .....
30236 DATA ....  ... .                    ........
30237 DATA ....    .  . .............    ......
30238 DATA ........  . .       .        ...  .....
30240 DATA ....           .  ....  . .    ..  .....
30242 DATA ....  .......       .  ...   .  .....
30243 DATA ....  .      .  ....  .  . ..  .  .....
30244 DATA ....  .  ...  .          .  .      .  .....
30246 DATA ....  .  .  .       ..    .  ....  .  .....
30248 DATA ....  .     . .  ....  .       .  .  .....
30250 DATA ....  .....  .    ..    ....  . .  .....
30252 DATA ....                .                .  .....
30254 DATA .....................................
30256 DATA .....................................
30258 DATA .....................................
30300 DATA .....................................
30302 DATA .....................................
30304 DATA ....  ..    .               .        .....
30306 DATA ....  ..   . .  ....  .  .. .    .....
30308 DATA ....        ..       ..   .   . . . .....
30310 DATA .....  ....  ...  .  .   . .    .....
30312 DATA .....           ..  .      .  . .....
30314 DATA ....      .  .  .  .  .  .  .  .......
30316 DATA .....  ..  .       .  .    -  .  . .....
30318 DATA ....     .  ..  ..        .  ..  .......
30320 DATA ....  .    .    .    .  -         .  .....
30322 DATA .....  .  .   .    .       ..  .  .  . .
30324 DATA ....  .   ..   .         .        .  .....
30326 DATA .....      . .....  ..  .  .    .....
30328 DATA ....  .  .  ..    . .        ...  ........
30330 DATA .....    ...      ...  ...       .  .....
30332 DATA .....  ..     ..  .  .    ..    ...  .....
30334 DATA ....    .   ..     .  ..    .   .  ......
30336 DATA ....  ..  .    ...  ....  ..  ..  .....
30338 DATA ....  ..  .  ..  .    .  .  ..  ..  .....
30340 DATA ....  ..  .         .  .        ..  .  .....
30342 DATA ....          .  ...  .    .  . ..  . ......
30344 DATA ....  ..  . ..      ...  . ..  .  .....
30346 DATA ....  ..  .    ..       ..  .  .   .....
30348 DATA ....  .....      ........  . ..  .......
30350 DATA ....  .      ..            .  . ..  .......
30352 DATA ....  .  ..     .......  . .       .....
30354 DATA ....  .  ..  .       ...    . ....  .....
30356 DATA ....     . ....        .             .....
30358 DATA .....................................
30360 DATA .....................................
30362 DATA .....................................
```

ChexSum Tables

1 = 2150	10190 = 965	30224 = 1460
2 = 115	15000 = 3412	30226 = 1488
3 = 2208	15010 = 2678	30228 = 1432
9 = 1484	15020 = 1173	30230 = 1488
10 = 1570	15030 = 3051	30232 = 1432
11 = 3124	15040 = 1182	30234 = 1502
12 = 3328	15060 = 1403	30236 = 1404
13 = 3340	15070 = 718	30237 = 1516
14 = 2767	15100 = 3126	30238 = 1446
31 = 5147	15110 = 2461	30240 = 1432
32 = 5312	20000 = 2673	30242 = 1474
33 = 4963	20100 = 115	30243 = 1460
34 = 2032	30100 = 1628	30244 = 1418
35 = 2479	30102 = 1628	30246 = 1474
36 = 4767	30104 = 1362	30248 = 1446
37 = 3925	30106 = 1488	30250 = 1502
38 = 2597	30108 = 1418	30252 = 1334
40 = 691	30110 = 1502	30254 = 1628
50 = 129	30112 = 1404	30256 = 1628
60 = 1216	30114 = 1544	30258 = 1628
80 = 336	30116 = 1390	30300 = 1628
100 = 1951	30118 = 1502	30302 = 1628
105 = 493	30120 = 1404	30304 = 1348
110 = 1212	30122 = 1558	30306 = 1468
120 = 2805	30124 = 1362	30308 = 1418
150 = 112	30126 = 1530	30310 = 1488
400 = 1540	30128 = 1390	30312 = 1404
410 = 1007	30130 = 1502	30314 = 1446
420 = 1437	30132 = 1432	30316 = 1446
430 = 58	30134 = 1474	30318 = 1418
1000 = 1401	30136 = 1488	30320 = 1390
1010 = 579	30138 = 1418	30322 = 1460
1020 = 441	30140 = 1516	30324 = 1390
1030 = 1267	30142 = 1404	30326 = 1474
1040 = 3868	30143 = 1460	30328 = 1474
1050 = 334	30144 = 1502	30330 = 1460
1060 = 2669	30145 = 1460	30332 = 1474
1070 = 2739	30146 = 1460	30334 = 1418
1100 = 58	30148 = 1432	30336 = 1502
10000 = 391	30150 = 1558	30338 = 1474
10010 = 1759	30152 = 1334	30340 = 1432
10020 = 2992	30154 = 1628	30342 = 1446
10021 = 1686	30156 = 1628	30344 = 1488
10100 = 4469	30158 = 1628	30346 = 1432
10110 = 4723	30200 = 1628	30348 = 1530
10120 = 3135	30202 = 1628	30350 = 1418
10121 = 4124	30204 = 1348	30352 = 1460
10122 = 4347	30206 = 1502	30354 = 1488
10123 = 3015	30208 = 1404	30356 = 1390
10130 = 4352	30210 = 1516	30358 = 1628
10135 = 1600	30212 = 1376	30360 = 1628
10140 = 4552	30214 = 1558	30362 = 1628
10150 = 4632	30216 = 1376	
10160 = 4624	30218 = 1558	
10170 = 4526	30220 = 1362	TOTAL = 298872
10180 = 1367	30222 = 1488	

LETRMAZE

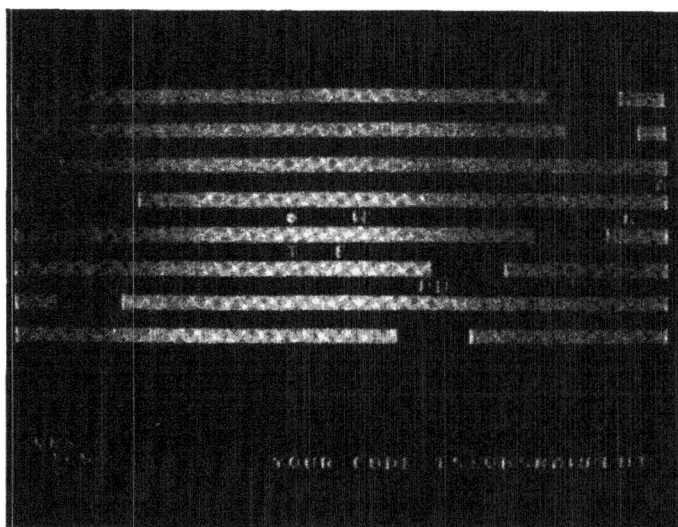

CLASSIFICATION: Skill

The object is to collect the letters in the maze in the shortest possible time and in the same order as shown at the bottom right of the screen. A letter is collected by touching it with your man. Joystick 2 moves your man (solid circle) vertically and horizontally. When the fire button is held down movement will be two spaces at once instead of one. Movement 'wraps around' horizontaly.

PROGRAMMING SUGGESTIONS

Increase the size of the maze and give a number of levels to the game.

Program Variables

A( )	Holds offsets
AM	=2 if fire pressed else =1
CODE$	Holds code to be done
D( )	Direction of line movement
MAX	Constant for random selection
OK	Flag
OLDPH	Old horizontal position
OLDPV	Old vertical position
PH	Man's horizontal position
PLACE	Points to next code letter to be obtained
POS	Screen address
PV	Man's vertical position
Q	Local
R	Where to peek for a random number
SCREEN	Address of first byte of video RAM
T	Local
TIME	Holds score
TN	Constant =39
X	Local
X$	Local string
Y	Local
Z	Local

Program Structure

10		Set margins and goto initialize
100 -	200	Draw the maze
300 -	350	Read the joystick routine
1000 -	1090	Main loop
2000 -	2040	Hit something
3000 -	3070	Wrong thing
4000 -	4030	Got all the pieces
20000 -	21000	Initialize subroutine

Listing

```
10    POKE 82.0:POKE 83.39:GOTO 20000
```

```
┌─────────────────────────────────────┐
│         Draw the maze               │
└─────────────────────────────────────┘
```

```
100   POSITION 0.1:Z=A(1):? B$(Z.Z+TN):Z=Z+D(1):IF Z>FE THEN
      Z=Z-FE
101   IF Z<1 THEN Z=Z+FE
102   A(1)=Z:IF PEEK(R)>MAX THEN D(1)=-D(1)
110   POSITION 0.3:Z=A(2):? B$(Z.Z+TN):Z=Z+D(2):IF Z>FE THEN
      Z=Z-FE
111   IF Z<1 THEN Z=Z+FE
112   A(2)=Z:IF PEEK(R)>MAX THEN D(2)=-D(2)
120   POSITION 0.5:Z=A(3):? B$(Z.Z+TN):Z=Z+D(3):IF Z>FE THEN
      Z=Z-FE
121   IF Z<1 THEN Z=Z+FE
122   A(3)=Z:IF PEEK(R)>MAX THEN D(3)=-D(3)
130   POSITION 0.7:Z=A(4):? B$(Z.Z+TN):Z=Z+D(4):IF Z>FE THEN
      Z=Z-FE
131   IF Z<1 THEN Z=Z+FE
132   A(4)=Z:IF PEEK(R)>MAX THEN D(4)=-D(4)
140   POSITION 0.9:Z=A(5):? B$(Z.Z+TN):Z=Z+D(5):IF Z>FE THEN
      Z=Z-FE
141   IF Z<1 THEN Z=Z+FE
142   A(5)=Z:IF PEEK(R)>MAX THEN D(5)=-D(5)
150   POSITION 0.11:Z=A(6):? B$(Z.Z+TN):Z=Z+D(6):IF Z>FE THEN
      Z=Z-FE
151   IF Z<1 THEN Z=Z+FE
152   A(6)=Z:IF PEEK(R)>MAX THEN D(6)=-D(6)
160   POSITION 0.13:Z=A(7):? B$(Z.Z+TN):Z=Z+D(7):IF Z>FE THEN
      Z=Z-FE
161   IF Z<1 THEN Z=Z+FE
162   A(7)=Z:IF PEEK(R)>MAX THEN D(7)=-D(7)
170   POSITION 0.15:Z=A(8):? B$(Z.Z+TN):Z=Z+D(8):IF Z>FE THEN
      Z=Z-FE
171   IF Z<1 THEN Z=Z+FE
172   A(8)=Z:IF PEEK(R)>MAX THEN D(8)=-D(8)
200   RETURN
```

```
┌─────────────────────────────────────┐
│    Read the joystick routine        │
└─────────────────────────────────────┘
```

```
300   Z=STICK(0):AM=1:IF  NOT STRIG(0) THEN AM=2
310   IF Z=14 AND PV>0 THEN PV=PV-AM
320   IF Z=13 AND PV<21 THEN PV=PV+AM
330   IF Z=11 THEN PH=PH-AM:IF PH<0 THEN PH=TN
340   IF Z=7 THEN PH=PH+AM:IF PH>TN THEN PH=0
350   RETURN
```

```
                    ┌─────────────────────────┐
                    │  Main loop              │
                    └─────────────────────────┘

1000    GOSUB 100:POSITION 2.23:? TIME;" ";:TIME=TIME+1
1010    GOSUB 300
1020    POS=PH+40*PV+SCREEN
1030    OLDPOS=OLDPH+40*OLDPV+SCREEN
1040    Q=PEEK(POS):IF Q THEN 2000
1050    POKE OLDPOS,0
1060    POKE POS,84
1070    OLDPH=PH:OLDPV=PV
1090    GOTO 1000

                    ┌─────────────────────────┐
                    │  Hit something          │
                    └─────────────────────────┘

2000    IF Q=84 THEN 1050
2010    IF ASC(CODE$(PLACE,PLACE))<>Q+32 THEN 3000
2020    POSITION PLACE,22:? CHR$(Q+32);
2030    PLACE=PLACE+1:IF PLACE=11 THEN 4000
2040    GOTO 1050

                    ┌─────────────────────────┐
                    │  Wrong thing            │
                    └─────────────────────────┘

3000    FOR T=1 TO 28:? :NEXT T
3010    ? "        NOPE YOU FLUFFED  T!"
3020    FOR T=1 TO 12:FOR X=1 TO 10:NEXT X:? :NEXT T
3030    FOR T=1 TO 1000:NEXT T
3040    POSITION 5,23
3050    ? "                                        ";
3060    INPUT X$
3070    RUN

                    ┌─────────────────────────┐
                    │  Got all the pieces     │
                    └─────────────────────────┘

4000    FOR T=1 TO 28:? :NEXT T
4010    ? "YOU HAVE COMPLETED THE CODE!"
4020    ? :? "YOUR TIME WAS ";TIME
4030    GOTO 3020
```

Initialize subroutine

```
20000 DIM B$(88),X$(9):R=53770:MAX=240:TN=39:FE=48
20010 GRAPHICS 2+16
20020 POSITION 7,6
20030 ? #6;"WAIT"
20040 FOR X=1 TO 40
20050 B$(X,X)=CHR$(160)
20060 NEXT X
20070 FOR X=41 TO 44
20080 B$(X,X)=" "
20090 NEXT X
20100 FOR X=45 TO 88
20110 B$(X,X)=CHR$(160)
20120 NEXT X
20130 DIM A(8),D(8)
20140 FOR X=1 TO 8
20150 Z=INT(RND(0)*35)+1
20160 A(X)=Z
20170 Z=INT(RND(0)*2)-1
20180 IF Z=0 THEN 20170
20190 D(X)=Z
20200 NEXT X
20220 DIM CODE$(10):SCREEN=40000
20230 FOR X=1 TO 10
20240 Z=INT(RND(0)*26)+65
20250 IF LEN(CODE$)=0 THEN 20300
20260 OK=1
20270 FOR T=1 TO LEN(CODE$)
20280 IF ASC(CODE$(T,T))=Z THEN OK=0
20290 NEXT T:IF NOT OK THEN 20240
20300 CODE$(X,X)=CHR$(Z)
20310 NEXT X
20320 GRAPHICS 0:POKE 752,255:GOSUB 100
20340 FOR T=1 TO LEN(CODE$)
20350 Y=INT(RND(0)*7)+2
20360 X=INT(RND(0)*40)
20370 OK=Y*40+X+SCREEN
```

Put character to screen

```
20380 IF PEEK(OK)>0 THEN 20350
20390 POKE OK,ASC(CODE$(T,T))-32
20410 NEXT T
20420 PLACE=1
20430 POSITION 16,23
20440 ? "YOUR CODE IS:";CODE$;
20450 PH=20:PV=21
20460 OLDPH=PH:OLDPV=PV
20470 TIME=0
21000 GOTO 1000
```

ChexSum Tables

```
10   = 906          1040  = 912         20140 = 414
100  = 3398         1050  = 227         20150 = 906
101  = 843          1060  = 421         20160 = 627
102  = 1939         1070  = 817         20170 = 852
110  = 3402         1090  = 127         20180 = 427
111  = 843          2000  = 620         20190 = 630
112  = 1942         2010  = 1288        20200 = 180
120  = 3406         2020  = 930         20220 = 757
121  = 843          2030  = 1041        20230 = 422
122  = 1945         2040  = 207         20240 = 987
130  = 3410         3000  = 738         20250 = 503
131  = 843          3010  = 1782        20260 = 351
132  = 1948         3020  = 1452        20270 = 641
140  = 3414         3030  = 626         20280 = 1278
141  = 843          3040  = 281         20290 = 592
142  = 1951         3050  = 6208        20300 = 1017
150  = 3424         3060  = 174         20310 = 180
151  = 843          3070  = 59          20320 = 666
152  = 1954         4000  = 738         20340 = 641
160  = 3428         4010  = 2022        20350 = 880
161  = 843          4020  = 1367        20360 = 818
162  = 1957         4030  = 191         20370 = 966
170  = 3432         20000 = 2766        20380 = 588
171  = 843          20010 = 282         20390 = 1155
172  = 1960         20020 = 254         20410 = 179
200  = 58           20030 = 523         20420 = 347
300  = 1520         20040 = 470         20430 = 298
310  = 1122         20050 = 1049        20440 = 1174
320  = 1216         20060 = 180         20450 = 763
330  = 1567         20070 = 538         20460 = 817
340  = 1551         20080 = 757         20470 = 274
350  = 58           20090 = 180         21000 = 127
1000 = 1317         20100 = 610
1010 = 116          20110 = 1049
1020 = 929          20120 = 180         TOTAL = 113175
1030 = 943          20130 = 695
```

BREAKIN

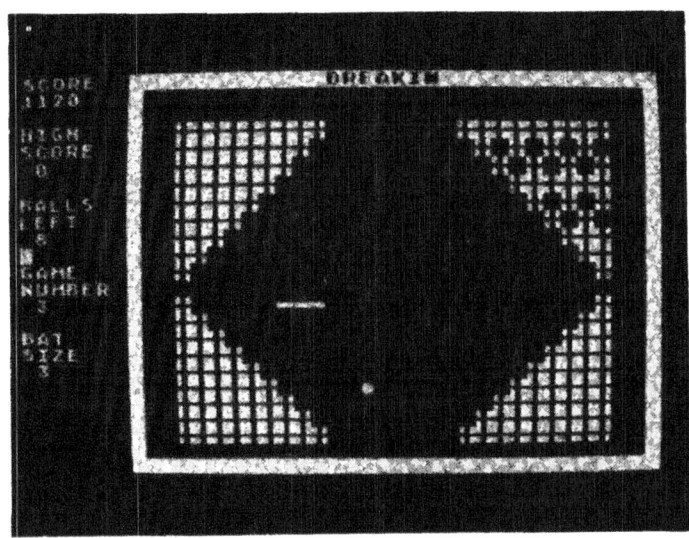

CLASSIFICATION: Reflex

You are inside a four-walled container with a series of brick walls, a moving ball and a bat. The ball is bouncing off the bricks and you must use your bat to stop it getting past you and hitting the wall. You are given nine balls for each game and you lose a ball each time one gets past your bat. The bat can be moved left and right using the joystick. There are three different bricks walls and two bat sizes. The smaller the bat, the more points scored.

PROGRAMMING SUGGESTIONS

Add more brick walls to the game and make them more exotic. Vary the speed that the ball travels round the court.

Program Variables

SC	Start of screen
KE	Joystick port value
BS	Batsize
GS	Game size
BV	Vertical postion of bat
BH	Horizontal position of bat
BY	Vertical position of ball
BX	Horizontal position of ball
BA	Screen position of ball
DX	Horizontal movement value of ball
DY	Vertical movement value of ball

Program Structure

10 -	55	Intialization
60 -	150	Move the bat across the screen
160 -	260	Check for boundary hit
270 -	310	Check for missed ball
320 -	810	Select the game
830 -	890	Print game one on the screen
900 -	980	Print game two on the screen
990 -	1080	Print game three on the screen
1090 -	1150	End the game

Listing

```
1       SETCOLOR 2,7,4
10      REM BREAKIN
11      CLR
12      DIM DN$(63),GM$(1),BS$(1),A$(1),SPC$(40)
13      SP=0:REM SET DEFINITION OF SPACE
14      POKE 82,0:BE=40000:REM START OF SCREEN
15      WI=82:REM SET BAT CHARACTER
16      WA=211:REM SET BARRIER CHARACTER
17      CI=84:REM SET BALL CHARACTER
19      POKE 752,0
20      DN$(1,63)="♦♦♦♦♦♦♦♦♦♦♦♦♦♦♦♦♦♦♦♦♦♦♦♦♦♦♦♦♦♦♦♦♦♦→→→→→→→
        →→→→→→→→→→→→→→→→→→→→"
21      FOR I=1 TO 40:SPC$(I,I)="→":NEXT I
30      SC=40000:NB=9:GOTO 330
40      GOTO 20
50      SOUND 0,60,10,8:SOUND 0,60,10,0
55      RETURN
60      REM MOVE BAT
61      REM ========
70      KE=STICK(1):IF KE=15 THEN A=64
80      IF KE=7 THEN A=12
90      IF KE=11 THEN A=36
100     IF A=64 THEN 170
110     PO=BE+(BV*40)+BH:FOR I=PO TO PO+BS-1:POKE I,0:NEXT I
120     BH=BH+((A=12)-(A=36))*2
130     IF BH<8 THEN BH=8
140     IF BH>38-BS THEN BH=38-BS
150     PO=BE+(BV*40)+BH:FOR I=PO TO PO+BS-1:POKE I,82:NEXT I
160     REM CHECK BOUNDARY HIT
161     REM =================
170     BX=BX+DX:BY=BY+DY:FF=21
180     IF BX<9 THEN DX=-DX:GOSUB 50:GOTO 230
190     IF BX>36 THEN DX=-DX:GOSUB 50:GOTO 230
200     IF BY<=1 THEN BY=1:DY=-DY:GOSUB 50:GOTO 230
210     IF BY>=22 THEN BY=22:DY=-DY:GOSUB 50
220     REM CHECK BAT/BRICK HIT & PRINT BALL
230     POKE BA,SP:BA=SC+BY*40+BX
240     IF PEEK(BA)=WI THEN BA=B1:DY=-DY:FF=-133:GOSUB 50:GOTO
        60
250     IF PEEK(BA)=WA THEN DY=-DY:FF=35:GOSUB 50:GS=GS+1:POSIT
        ION 0,0:PRINT "♦";GS
260     POKE BA,CI
270     REM CHECK FOR MISSED BALL
280     IF GM=1 AND BY=22 AND DY=-1 THEN NB=NB-1:POSITION 0,0:P
        RINT "♦♦♦♦♦♦♦♦♦";"▲";NB
290     IF GM<>1 AND BY=11 THEN NB=NB-1:POSITION 0,0:PRINT "♦♦♦
        ♦♦♦♦♦♦";"▲";NB
300     IF NB<1 THEN 1090
310     IF INT(GS/100)-(GS/100)<>0 THEN 60
320     ON GM GOSUB 830,900,990
330     REM
340     PRINT CHR$(125);
600     PRINT CHR$(125);:PRINT "♦♦♦♦♦♦♦♦♦♦▲▲▲▲▲▲▲▲▲▲
        ▲B▲R▲E▲A▲K▲I▲N"
```

```
610   FOR I=1 TO 200:NEXT I:FF=21:PRINT "♦♦"
620   GOSUB 50
630   PRINT "▲▲▲▲▲▲▲▲SELECT GAME NUMBER(1-3)":FOR
      T=1 TO 90:N EXT T
640   PRINT "♦▲▲▲▲▲▲▲▲SELECT▲GAME▲NUMBER(1-3)";:FOR T=1
      TO 90 :NEXT T
650   GM=PEEK(754):IF GM<26 THEN PRINT :PRINT "♦";:GOTO 620
660   IF GM>31 THEN PRINT :PRINT "♦";:GOTO 620
661   IF GM=31 THEN GM=1:GOTO 670
662   IF GM=30 THEN GM=2:GOTO 670
663   IF GM=26 THEN GM=3:GOTO 670
665   GOTO 640
670   PRINT "▲";GM:PRINT :FF=35
675   POKE 754,0
680   GOSUB 50
690   PRINT "▲▲▲▲▲▲▲▲▲SELECT BAT SIZE(2-3)":FOR T=1
      TO 90:NEXT
700   PRINT "♦▲▲▲▲▲▲▲▲▲SELECT▲BAT▲SIZE(2-3)";:FOR T=1
      TO 90:NEXT T
710   BS=PEEK(754):IF BS<26 THEN PRINT :PRINT "♦";:GOTO 680
720   IF BS>30 THEN PRINT :PRINT "♦";:GOTO 680
721   IF BS=30 THEN BS=2:GOTO 730
722   IF BS=26 THEN BS=3:GOTO 730
725   GOTO 700
730   POKE 754,0:PRINT "▲";BS
740   NB=9:GS=100*(4-BS)
750   FOR T=1 TO 500:NEXT T
760   PRINT CHR$(125);:PRINT "▲▲▲▲▲▲▲▲ BREAKIN "
770   FOR I=1 TO 22:PRINT "▲▲▲▲▲▲▲■▲▲▲▲▲▲▲▲▲▲
      ▲▲▲▲▲▲▲▲▲▲▲■":NEXT I
780   PRINT "▲▲▲▲▲▲▲▲ ";::POSITION 0,0
790   POSITION 0,0:PRINT "SCORE":PRINT "";GS:PRINT "♦HIGH":PR
      INT "SCORE":PRINT "▲";HS:PRINT "♦BALLS"
800   PRINT "LEFT":PRINT "▲";NB:PRINT "♦GAME":PRINT "NUMBER":
      PRINT "▲";GM
810   PRINT "♦BAT":PRINT "SIZE":PRINT "▲";BS
820   ON GM GOTO 830,900,990
830   REM GAME 1
840   POSITION 0,0:PRINT "♦♦"
850   FOR J=1 TO 4:PRINT "→→→→→→→→:==================
      ==========":NEXT J
860   IF GS>0 THEN GS=GS+1
870   IF SW>0 THEN 60
880   SW=1:BV=21:BH=17:BY=15:BX=18:BA=SC+BY*40+BX:DX=-1:DY=-1
890   GOTO 110
900   REM GAME2
910   POSITION 0,0:PRINT "♦♦"
920   FOR J=1 TO 3:PRINT "→→→→→→→→:==================
      :===:":NEXT J
930   PRINT "♦♦♦♦♦♦♦♦♦♦♦♦♦"
940   FOR J=1 TO 3:PRINT "→→→→→→→→:==================
      :===:":NEXT J
950   IF GS>0 THEN GS=GS+1
960   IF SW>0 THEN 60
```

```
970   SW=1:BV=13:BH=20:BY=10:BX=21:BA=SC+BY*40+BX:DX=1:DY=-1
980   GOTO 110
990   REM GAME 3
1000  POSITION 0,0:PRINT "↓↓"
1010  FOR I=0 TO 8:PRINT "→→→→→→→→→→";:FOR J=9-I TO 1 STEP
      -1 :PRINT "::";:NEXT J
1020  PRINT SPC$(1,I*2+8);:FOR J=9-I TO 1 STEP -1:PRINT "::";:
      NEXT J:PRINT :NEXT I:PRINT
1030  FOR I=0 TO 8:PRINT "→→→→→→→→→→";:FOR J=1
      TO I+1:PRINT "::";:NEXT J
1040  PRINT SPC$(1,((8-I)*2)+8);:FOR J=1 TO I+1:PRINT "::";:NE
      XT J:PRINT :NEXT I:POSITION 0,0
1050  IF GS>0 THEN GS=GS+1
1060  IF SW>0 THEN 60
1070  SW=1:BV=13:BH=16:BY=9:BX=24:BA=SC+BY*40+BX:DX=1:DY=-1
1080  GOTO 110
1090  REM END OF GAME
1100  POSITION 0,0:PRINT "↓↓↓↓↓↓↓↓↓↓↓↓↓↓↓↓↓→→→→→→→→→→...
      ▲ANOTHER▲ GAME(Y/N)";
1110  INPUT A$
1120  IF A$="N" THEN PRINT CHR$(125);:END
1130  IF A$<>"Y" THEN 1110
1140  IF GS>HS THEN HS=GS
1150  SW=0:GOTO 600
```

ChexSum Tables

1 = 353	290 = 1987	810 = 1020
11 = 40	300 = 546	820 = 721
12 = 1835	310 = 1127	840 = 268
13 = 2052	320 = 722	850 = 5505
14 = 1926	340 = 356	860 = 809
15 = 1820	600 = 1689	870 = 436
16 = 2019	610 = 1185	880 = 4055
17 = 1893	620 = 192	890 = 128
19 = 253	630 = 5639	910 = 268
20 = 2648	640 = 2749	920 = 5504
21 = 1436	650 = 1424	930 = 429
30 = 914	660 = 745	940 = 5504
40 = 142	661 = 996	950 = 809
50 = 985	662 = 996	960 = 436
55 = 58	663 = 987	970 = 3998
70 = 1344	665 = 181	980 = 128
80 = 680	670 = 771	1000 = 268
90 = 726	675 = 255	1010 = 2193
100 = 602	680 = 192	1020 = 2740
110 = 2387	690 = 5073	1030 = 1998
120 = 1443	700 = 2567	1040 = 2962
130 = 676	710 = 1502	1050 = 809
140 = 1145	720 = 831	1060 = 436
150 = 2581	721 = 915	1070 = 3984
170 = 1635	722 = 906	1080 = 128
180 = 1216	725 = 118	1100 = 2269
190 = 1262	730 = 551	1110 = 155
200 = 1621	740 = 1129	1120 = 761
210 = 1476	750 = 631	1130 = 452
230 = 1341	760 = 6151	1140 = 825
240 = 2462	770 = 2344	1150 = 434
250 = 2820	780 = 5650	
260 = 360	790 = 2712	TOTAL = 152964
280 = 2460	800 = 1962	

RACER

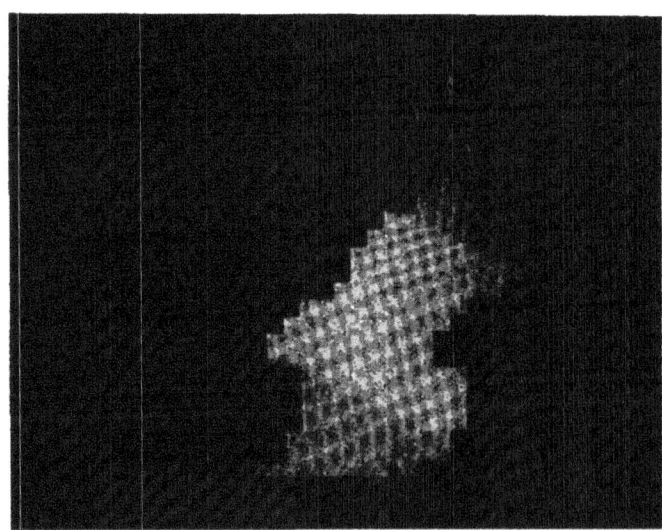

CLASSIFICATION: Skill

The object of this game is to get as far around the course as possible. Steer the car left and right with the joystick. To make the car go faster push the joystick forward, to go slower press the joystick back.

PROGRAMMING SUGGESTIONS

Add a speedometer to the car so you can tell just how fast the car is travelling. Also add other cars to the race to compete against you.

Program Variables

A	Local
CAR$	Holds car
CARPOS	Horizontal position of car
DIFFICULTY	Difficulty level
F	Flag
LEFTLIMIT	Left limit of road
R	=53770 Where to peek for a random number 0 - 255
RIGHTLIMIT	Right limit of road
ROAD$	Holds road
ROADPOS	Horizontal position of road
SCORE	Holds score
SPEED	Speed of movement
VOL	Volume of sound
X	Local
Y	Local

Program Structure

10	Jump to initialization
300 - 610	Main loop
1000 - 1060	Game End
2000 - 2080	Game start
20000 - 21220	Initialize game

Listing

```
10      GOTO 20000
```

Main loop

```
300     SCORE=SCORE+1:X=RND(0)*DIFFICULTY:IF PEEK(R)>127 THEN X
        =-X
320     ROADPOS=ROADPOS+X:IF ROADPOS>RIGHTLIMIT THEN ROADPOS=RI
        GHTLIMIT
330     IF ROADPOS<LEFTLIMIT THEN ROADPOS=LEFTLIMIT
350     POSITION 1,0:? ROAD$(ROADPOS,ROADPOS+37):A=USR(ADR(CODE
        $))
360     IF PEEK(R)>217 THEN POKE 40041+INT(RND(0)*36),128
430     X=STICK(1):IF (X=11 OR X=10 OR X=9) AND CARPOS>3 THEN C
        ARPOS=CARPOS-1
440     IF (X=7 OR X=6 OR X=5) AND CARPOS<37 THEN CARPOS=CARPOS
        +1
450     IF PEEK(40920+CARPOS) THEN 1000
550     POSITION CARPOS,23:? CAR$;
560     SOUND 0,SPEED+40,2,8
570     IF (X=14 OR X=10 OR X=6) AND SPEED>0 THEN SPEED=SPEED-1
590     IF (X=13 OR X=9 OR X=5) AND SPEED<215 THEN SPEED=SPEED+
        1
600     IF SPEED=0 THEN 300
610     FOR X=1 TO SPEED STEP 4:NEXT X:GOTO 300
```

Game End

```
1000    VOL=15:FOR Y=0 TO 4:FOR X=0 TO 32:POSITION CARPOS,23
1010    ? CHR$(X);:SOUND 0,20,0,VOL:VOL=VOL-0.09:NEXT X:NEXT Y
1020    FOR X=0 TO 25:? :NEXT X
1030    ? "SCORE= ";SCORE:? :? :? "AT LEVEL :";DIFFICULTY:? :?
1040    ? :? :? "PRESS START FOR ANOTHER GAME"
1050    IF PEEK(53279)<>6 THEN 1050
1060    GOTO 21000
```

Game start

```
2000    POKE 752,1:? CHR$(125):FOR X=1 TO 30:POSITION 1,0:? ROA
        D$(16,53);:A=USR(ADR(CODE$)):NEXT X
2010    CARPOS=22:POSITION CARPOS,23:? CAR$;:SOUND 0,240,2,8
2020    POSITION 17,18:? "■START■";
2030    GOSUB 21200:IF  NOT STRIG(1) THEN 2070
2040    POSITION 17,18:? "■START■";
2050    GOSUB 21200:IF  NOT STRIG(1) THEN 2070
2060    GOTO 2020
```

```
2070    POSITION 17,18:? "▲▲▲▲▲▲▲"::POSITION 18,19:? "▲▲▲▲▲
        ▲";:
        POSITION CARPOS,23:? "▲":
2080    GOTO 300
```

> Initialize game

```
20000 POKE 82,1:? CHR$(125):DIM ROAD$(120),CAR$(1)
20010 ROAD$="███████████████████████████████████▲▲▲▲▲▲
      ▲▲▲▲████████████████████████████████"
20020 CAR$=CHR$(123)
20030 LEFTLIMIT=4
20040 RIGHTLIMIT=30
20050 DIM CODE$(58)
20060 DATA 104,169,176,133,203,169,159,133,204,169,216,133,20
      5,169,159,133,206,162,22,160
20061 DATA 40,177,203,145,205,136,16,249,165,203,56,233,40,13
      3,203,165,204,233,0
20062 DATA 133,204,165,205,56,233,40,133,205,165,206,233,0,13
      3,206,202,16,218,96
20080 FOR X=1 TO 58:READ Y:CODE$(X,X)=CHR$(Y):NEXT X
20090 SETCOLOR 4,8,6
20100 SETCOLOR 2,4,15
21000 POKE 752,0:? :? :? "████████████████RACER████████
      ████████"
21010 ? :? :? :? "SELECT▲DIFFICULTY▲LEVEL▲(▲1-5)"::INPUT DIFF
      ICULTY
21020 IF DIFFICULTY AND DIFFICULTY>5 THEN ? :? "PLEASE▲....."
      :GOTO 21010
21021 ? :? "STEER▲CAR▲WITH▲JOYSTICK▲2"
21022 ? :? "FORWARD▲=▲FASTER▲▲BACK▲=▲SLOWER":?
21030 ? :? "PRESS▲FIRE▲BUTTON▲TO▲START▲CAR▲MOVING":? :?
21040 ROADPOS=16
21050 SPEED=215
21060 R=53770
21100 POSITION 14,23
21110 ? "█PRESS▲START";
21120 GOSUB 21200:IF F THEN 2000
21130 POSITION 14,23
21140 ? "█PRESS▲START";
21150 GOSUB 21200:IF F THEN 2000
21160 GOTO 21100
21200 F=0:FOR X=0 TO 100
21210 IF PEEK(53279)=6 THEN F=1
21220 NEXT X:RETURN
```

ChexSum Tables

```
   10 = 114              2000 = 3257         21010 = 2516
  300 = 2154             2010 = 1499         21020 = 1553
  320 = 1307             2020 = 1143         21021 = 1917
  330 = 734              2030 = 751          21022 = 2364
  350 = 1780             2040 = 1783         21030 = 3045
  360 = 1447             2050 = 751          21040 = 353
  430 = 2425             2060 = 175          21050 = 363
  440 = 1863             2070 = 1969         21060 = 504
  450 = 623              2080 = 114          21100 = 296
  550 = 576             20000 = 1520         21110 = 2505
  560 = 625             20010 = 10262        21120 = 467
  570 = 1776            20020 = 540          21130 = 296
  590 = 1853            20030 = 337          21140 = 1097
  600 = 326             20040 = 380          21150 = 467
  610 = 894             20050 = 448          21160 = 131
 1000 = 1557            20060 = 4020         21200 = 634
 1010 = 1843            20061 = 3547         21210 = 959
 1020 = 632             20062 = 3545         21220 = 226
 1030 = 2001            20080 = 1921
 1040 = 2241            20090 = 358
 1050 = 773             20100 = 367         TOTAL = 92784
 1060 = 130             21000 = 6730
```

ROCKS

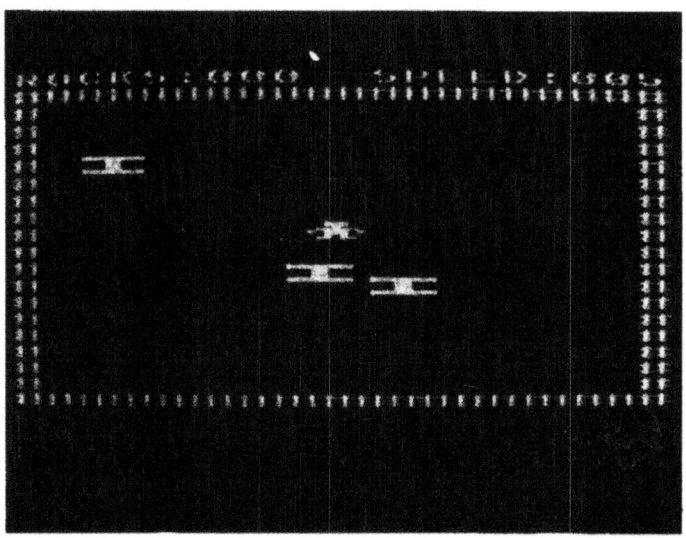

CLASSIFICATION: Evasion

Move your ship round the room without crashing into the nasty monsters bouncing off the walls. Every time you hit one the computer will print BANG. Try to live as long as possible

PROGRAMMING SUGGESTIONS

Put obstacles in the path of you and the monsters. Increase the speed of the game.

Program Variables

I	General purpose
X1	X co-ordinate of you
Y1	Y co-ordinate of you
X2	X co-ordinate of rock one
Y2	Y co-ordinate of rock one
X3	X co-ordinate of rock two
Y3	Y co-ordinate of rock two
X4	X co-ordinate of rock three
Y4	Y co-ordinate of rock three

Program Structure

```
   2 -   85 Initialize the program
 100 -  130 Data for players
 200 -  630 Set up sprites
1000 - 1040 Main loop
2000 - 2205 Move your player
3000 - 5999 Move the rocks
7000 - 8000 Do collision testing
9000 - 9090 Data for machine language program
```

Listing

```
2    CLR
6    FOR I=30720 TO 30799:READ A:POKE I,A:NEXT I
7    FOR I=33792 TO 33792+1023:POKE I,0:NEXT I
9    FOR I=28672 TO 29050:READ A:POKE I,A:NEXT I
10   POKE 106,128
20   PM=PEEK(106):PMBASE=PM*256
30   GRAPHICS 1
40   POKE 559,62
50   POKE 53277,3
60   POKE 54279,PM
70   POKE 53256,2
80   POKE 704,77:POKE 705,77:POKE 706,77
85   POKE 707,77
100  DATA 56,56,16,124,186,56,40,108,0,0,0,0,0,0,0,0,0,0,0,0
110  DATA 255,255,24,24,24,24,255,255,0,0,0,0,0,0,0,0,0,0,0,0
120  DATA 255,255,24,24,24,24,255,255,0,0,0,0,0,0,0,0,0,0,0,0
130  DATA 255,255,24,24,24,24,255,255,0,0,0,0,0,0,0,0,0,0,0,0
200  POKE 53256,1
210  POKE 53257,1
220  POKE 53258,1
230  POKE 53259,1
500  X1=140:Y1=100:REM SET PLAYER COOR
510  X2=INT(RND(0)*150):Y2=INT(RND(0)*150)
520  XP2=4:YP2=4
530  X3=INT(RND(0)*150):Y3=INT(RND(1)*150)
540  XP3=4:YP3=4
550  X4=INT(RND(0)*150):Y4=INT(RND(1)*150)
560  XP4=4:YP4=4
570  A=USR(28672,X1,Y1,X2,Y2,X3,Y3,X4,Y4)
600  FOR I=32128 TO 32128+19:POKE I,3:NEXT I
610  FOR I=32128+380 TO 32128+380+19:POKE I,3:NEXT I
620  FOR I=32128 TO 32128+380 STEP 20:POKE I,3:NEXT I
630  FOR I=32128+19 TO 32128+380 STEP 20:POKE I,3:NEXT I
1000 GOSUB 2000:REM MOVE YOU
1010 GOSUB 3000:REM MOVE 1
1020 GOSUB 4000:REM MOVE 2
1030 GOSUB 5000:REM MOVE 3
1035 A=USR(28672,X1,Y1,X2,Y2,X3,Y3,X4,Y4)
1037 GOSUB 7000
1040 GOTO 1000
2000 REM MOVE YOUR PLAYER
2010 POKE 53278,0:A=STICK(1)
2020 IF A=11 THEN GOSUB 2100
2030 IF A=7 THEN GOSUB 2200
2040 RETURN
2100 IF X1<5 THEN RETURN
2105 X1=X1-4:RETURN
2200 IF X1>140 THEN RETURN
2205 X1=X1+4:RETURN
3000 REM MOVE ROCK ONE
3005 IF X2>140 THEN XP2=-4
```

```
3010 IF X2<5 THEN XP2=4
3015 IF Y2>155 THEN YP2=-4
3020 IF Y2<5 THEN YP2=4
3025 X2=X2+XP2:Y2=Y2+YP2:RETURN
4000 REM MOVE ROCK TWO
4005 IF X3>140 THEN XP3=-4
4010 IF X3<5 THEN XP3=4
4015 IF Y3>155 THEN YP3=-4
4020 IF Y3<5 THEN YP3=4
4025 X3=X3+XP3:Y3=Y3+YP3:RETURN
4999 RETURN
5000 REM MOVE ROCK THREE
5005 IF X4>140 THEN XP4=-4
5010 IF X4<5 THEN XP4=4
5015 IF Y4>155 THEN YP4=-4
5020 IF Y4<5 THEN YP4=4
5025 X4=X4+XP4:Y4=Y4+YP4:RETURN
5999 RETURN
7000 REM
7010 IF PEEK(53260)<>0 THEN GOSUB 8000
7020 RETURN
8000 POSITION 0,0:PRINT #6;"":PRINT #6;"#▲▲▲▲▲▲▲▲BANG"
8010 FOR I=1 TO 200:NEXT I:POSITION 0,1:PRINT #6;"#▲▲▲▲▲▲▲▲
     ▲▲▲▲▲▲▲▲▲▲";
8020 POKE 53278,0:RETURN
9000 DATA 104,104,104,141,61,113,104,104,141,60,113,104,104,
     141,75,113,104,104,141,74
9005 DATA 113,104,104,141,89,113,104,104,141,88,113,104,104,
     141,103,113,104,104,141,102
9010 DATA 113,32,45,112,96,120,32,8,113,160,14,162,0,189,53,
     113,149,176,232,136
9015 DATA 208,247,32,170,112,160,14,162,0,181,176,157,53,113
     ,232,136,208,247,160,14
9020 DATA 162,0,189,67,113,149,176,232,136,208,247,32,170,11
     2,160,14,162,0,181,176
9025 DATA 157,67,113,232,136,208,247,160,14,162,0,189,81,113
     ,149,176,232,136,208,247
9030 DATA 32,170,112,160,14,162,0,181,176,157,81,113,232,136
     ,208,247,160,14,162,0
9035 DATA 189,95,113,149,176,232,136,208,247,32,170,112,160,
     14,162,0,181,176,157,95
9040 DATA 113,232,136,208,247,32,22,113,88,96,165,183,197,18
     2,240,68,160,0,165,184
9045 DATA 24,105,46,145,176,169,32,24,101,182,168,166,185,16
     9,0,145,178,200,202,16
9050 DATA 250,169,32,24,101,183,141,116,113,162,0,142,109,11
     3,166,185,172,109,113,177
9055 DATA 180,238,109,113,172,116,113,145,178,238,116,113,20
     2,16,237,165,183,133,182,165
9060 DATA 184,133,189,96,165,184,197,189,208,182,96,173,112,
     113,41,15,170,189,36,113
9065 DATA 238,112,113,96,160,14,162,0,181,176,157,117,113,23
     2,136,208,247,96,160,14
9070 DATA 162,0,189,117,113,149,176,232,136,208,247,96,1,2,3
     ,4,5,10,7,8
9075 DATA 7,8,11,4,2,4,1,4,8,0,208,0,132,0,120,0,0,0,8,0
```

```
9080  DATA 16,0,0,1,208,0,133,20,120,0,0,0,8,0,16,0,0,2,208,0
9085  DATA 134,40,120,0,0,0,8,0,16,0,0,3,208,0,135,60,120,0,0
      ,0
9090  DATA 8,0,0,0,0,0,0,79,0,0,0,0,0,0,0,141,30,208
```

ChexSum Tables

2 = 40	620 = 1464	5020 = 667
6 = 1356	630 = 1620	5025 = 1270
7 = 1421	1000 = 918	5999 = 58
9 = 1627	1010 = 728	7010 = 756
10 = 277	1020 = 745	7020 = 58
20 = 1124	1030 = 762	8000 = 1160
30 = 144	1035 = 2321	8010 = 1723
40 = 420	1037 = 225	8020 = 420
50 = 406	1040 = 127	9000 = 3800
60 = 473	2010 = 887	9005 = 3900
70 = 372	2020 = 463	9010 = 3548
80 = 1169	2030 = 454	9015 = 3747
85 = 361	2040 = 58	9020 = 3711
100 = 2555	2100 = 357	9025 = 3824
110 = 2600	2105 = 581	9030 = 3638
120 = 2600	2200 = 419	9035 = 3778
130 = 2600	2205 = 580	9040 = 3730
200 = 371	3005 = 766	9045 = 3719
210 = 372	3010 = 649	9050 = 3845
220 = 373	3015 = 789	9055 = 4013
230 = 374	3020 = 651	9060 = 3852
500 = 2022	3025 = 1222	9065 = 3760
510 = 1696	4005 = 774	9070 = 3163
520 = 704	4010 = 657	9075 = 2355
530 = 1769	4015 = 797	9080 = 2537
540 = 712	4020 = 659	9085 = 2637
550 = 1777	4025 = 1246	9090 = 2191
560 = 720	4999 = 58	
570 = 2321	5005 = 782	
600 = 1205	5010 = 665	TOTAL = 130781
610 = 1731	5015 = 805	

SNOWBALL

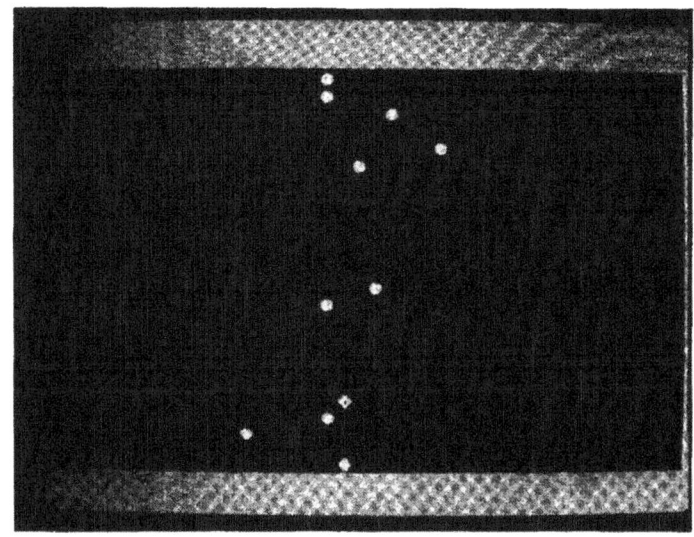

CLASSIFICATION: Evasion

Use joystick to move the man left and right. Shoot snowballs before they land by pressing the fire button.

PROGRAMMING SUGGESTIONS

Make the snowballs travel down the screen in random paths instead of straigh lines.

Program Variables

A	Local to set up USR routine
BALL$	Code for snowballs
BALLPOS	Ball position
CODE$	Holds machine code screen scroll routine
DIR	Direction group moves
FIREFLAG	=1 if missile fired
GROUP	Base position for snowballs
HITS	Counts hits
L	Local
LEVEL	Difficulty level
MISSILE$	String for missile
MISSX	Missile X co-ordinate
MISSY	Missile Y co-ordinate
PLAYERPOS	Position of player
SCORE	Score
SCREEN	Address of first byte of video RAM
SPACE$	40 spaces
T	Local
X	Local

Program Structure

1 - 3	Set the colors
10	Switch off cursor and jump to initialize
100 - 280	Main loop
1000 - 1060	The hit routine
2000 - 2060	The die routine
3000	Overrun by a snowball
3010 - 3030	Start the game
20000 - 21010	Initialize the game

Listing

```
1     SETCOLOR 1,0,15
2     SETCOLOR 4,0,9
3     SETCOLOR 2,0,0
10    POKE 752,1:POKE 82,0:GOTO 20000
```

Main loop

```
100   POSITION 0,0:? SPACE$
102   GROUP=GROUP+DIR:IF GROUP<0 THEN GROUP=0:DIR=-DIR
103   IF GROUP>29 THEN GROUP=29:DIR=-DIR
110   IF LEVEL>RND(0)*20 THEN POSITION RND(0)*10+GROUP,0:? BA
      LL$;:HITS=HITS-1:IF HITS<0 THEN 3000
130   X=STICK(1):IF X=11 AND PLAYERPOS>1 THEN PLAYERPOS=PLAYE
      RPOS-1
140   IF X=7 AND PLAYERPOS<38 THEN PLAYERPOS=PLAYERPOS+1
150   IF ( NOT STRIG(1)) AND ( NOT FIREFLAG) THEN FIREFLAG=1:
      MISSX=PLAYERPOS:MISSY=22
```

Put missile if required

```
200   IF FIREFLAG THEN POKE SCREEN+MISSX+40*MISSY,0
210   A=USR(ADR(CODE$))
220   IF PEEK(SCREEN+920+PLAYERPOS) THEN 2000
230   POKE SCREEN+920+PLAYERPOS,123
240   IF FIREFLAG AND PEEK(SCREEN+MISSX+(40*MISSY)) THEN GOSU
      B 1000
250   IF FIREFLAG THEN MISSY=MISSY-1:IF MISSY=-1 THEN FIREFLA
      G=0
260   IF FIREFLAG AND PEEK(SCREEN+MISSX+(40*MISSY)) THEN GOSU
      B 1000
270   IF FIREFLAG THEN POKE SCREEN+MISSX+40*MISSY,80
280   GOTO 100
```

The hit routine

```
1000  L=SCREEN+MISSX+40*MISSY:FOR X=0 TO 32
1020  POKE L,X
1040  SOUND 0,255-7*X,10,8
1050  NEXT X:SOUND 0,0,0,0:POKE L,0
1060  HITS=HITS+1:SCORE=SCORE+1:FIREFLAG=0:RETURN
```

The die routine

```
2000  FOR X=0 TO 255:SOUND 0,X,10,8:SOUND 1,X+128,10,8:SOUND
      2,X+2,10,8:SOUND 3,X+3,10,8:NEXT X
2010  FOR X=255 TO 0 STEP -6:SOUND 0,X,10,8:SOUND 1,X+1,10,8:
      NEXT X
2020  FOR X=0 TO 3:SOUND X,0,0,0:NEXT X
2030  FOR X=15 TO 0 STEP -1:SOUND 0,50,0,X:FOR Y=1 TO 4:NEXT
      Y:NEXT X
2040  FOR X=0 TO 23:? :NEXT X
2050  ? :? :? "A▴SNOWBALL▴HAS▴LANDED▴ON▴YOUR▴HEAD":? :? "AND▴
      YOUR▴BRAIN▴FREEZES":FOR X=1 TO 1000:NEXT X
2060  ? :? :? "SCORE▴";SCORE:? :? "LEVEL▴";LEVEL:? :? :GOTO 3
      010
```

Overrun by a snowball

```
3000  FOR X=1 TO 30:? :NEXT X:? CHR$(125):? :? :? :? "60▴SNOW
      BALLS▴HAVE▴LANDED":? :? :? "SCORE=";SCORE:? :? "AT▴LEVE
      L▴";LEVEL
3010  ? :? "PRESS▴FIRE▴FOR▴ANOTHER▴GAME"
3020  IF STRIG(1) THEN 3020
3030  RUN
```

Initialize the game

```
20000 DIM CODE$(58),BALL$(1),SPACE$(40),MISSILE$(1)
20011 BALLPOS=20:BALL$=CHR$(20):MISSILE$=CHR$(16)
20012 SPACE$="▴▴▴▴▴▴▴▴▴▴▴▴▴▴▴▴▴▴▴▴▴▴▴▴▴▴▴▴▴▴▴▴▴▴▴
      ▴▴▴▴▴"
20013 SCREEN=40000
20014 DIR=0.25
20015 SCORE=0
20016 HITS=60
20030 REM
20040 ? CHR$(125)
20041 ? :? :? :? "LEVEL▴";:INPUT LEVEL:? :?
20050 ? "USE▴JOYSTICK▴2":? :? :? "PRESS▴FIRE▴TO▴START▴GAME"
20060 DATA 104,169,176,133,203,169,159,133,204,169,216,133,20
      5,169,159,133,206,162,22,160
20061 DATA 40,177,203,145,205,136,16,249,165,203,56,233,40,13
      3,203,165,204,233,0
20062 DATA 133,204,165,205,56,233,40,133,205,165,206,233,0,13
      3,206,202,16,218,96
20070 FOR X=1 TO 58:READ T:CODE$(X,X)=CHR$(T):NEXT X
21000 IF STRIG(1) THEN 21000
21001 PLAYERPOS=20:FIREFLAG=0
21002 ? CHR$(125)
21003 IF  NOT STRIG(1) THEN 21003
21010 GOTO 100
```

ChexSum Tables

```
    1 = 298              280 = 112           20012 = 1585
    2 = 289             1000 = 1344          20013 = 344
    3 = 214             1020 = 347           20014 = 365
   10 = 809             1040 = 779           20015 = 278
  100 = 326             1050 = 664           20016 = 428
  102 = 1550            1060 = 1469          20040 = 343
  103 = 1178            2000 = 3558          20041 = 1103
  110 = 2481            2010 = 2082          20050 = 3057
  130 = 1704            2020 = 898           20060 = 4020
  140 = 1176            2030 = 2001          20061 = 3547
  150 = 1959            2040 = 640           20062 = 3545
  200 = 952             2050 = 5158          20070 = 1955
  210 = 736             2060 = 2006          21000 = 419
  220 = 807             3000 = 5400          21001 = 662
  230 = 654             3010 = 2063          21002 = 343
  240 = 1302            3020 = 480           21003 = 462
  250 = 1393            3030 = 59            21010 = 112
  260 = 1302           20000 = 1520
  270 = 1144           20011 = 1507          TOTAL = 74929
```

HUNTER

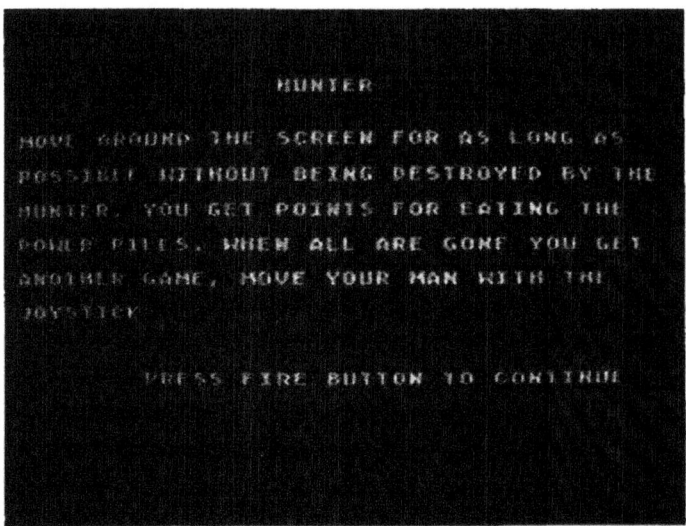

CLASSIFICATION: Invader/Evasion

You are a wild animal being pursued by a hunter. You move around the maze using the joystick on port one. No matter where you are in the maze, the hunter will know where you are and seek you out. As you move through the maze you eat munchies. When you have eaten all the munchies, you win. There are four levels.

PROGRAMMING SUGGESTIONS

Add a facility at the hardest level of the game so that the player can 'teleport' to another part of the board. However make it so that he cannot control his destination.

Program
Variables

JL	Screen value of block character
SP	Screen value of blank character
DO	Screen value of power pill
C1	Column position of hunter
R1	Row position of hunter
R	Row position of animal
C	Column position of animal
A	Joystick direction
CN	Number of power pills eaten

Program
Structure

15 -	40	Initialization
50 -	200	Draw borders, maze and power pills
210 -	560	Move your piece up, down, left and right
570 -	870	You ran into the hunter; you won the game

Listing

```
1       SETCOLOR 2,1,3:POKE 752,1
```

> Initialization

```
15      CLR :DIM A$(4),B$(1),C$(3),E$(3),CC$(40),RR$(24),DR$(1)
        ,TAB$(40),F$(32)
16      DIM D$(30)
20      PRINT CHR$(125);
21      POKE 82,0
22      DR$(1)="→":JL=128:REM SET BLOCK CHARACTER
23      SP=0:REM SET ASCII VALUE OF SPACE CHARACTER
24      DO=84:REM ASCII VALUE OF POWER FILL
25      FOR I=1 TO 40:TAB$(I,I)=DR$:NEXT I
26      YO=10:REM ASCII VALUE OF YOUR PLAYER
27      MO=56:REM ASCII VALUE OF MONSTER
30      GOSUB 710
40      GOSUB 850
```

> Draw borders, maze and power pills

```
50      PRINT CHR$(125);
60      SC=40000:CO=0:BE=SC+207
70      A$(1,2)="■":B$(1,1)=" ":C$(1,2)=A$:C$(3,3)=B$
80      E$(1,3)=" ●"
90      FOR I=1 TO 40:CC$(I,I)="→":NEXT I
100     FOR I=1 TO 24:RR$(I,I)="↓":NEXT I
110     FOR I=SC TO SC+39:POKE I,128:POKE I+920,128:NEXT I
120     FOR I=SC TO SC+999 STEP 40:POKE I,128:POKE I+39,128:NEX
        T I
130     POSITION 0,0:PRINT TAB$(1,18);"HUNTER";
140     FOR I=1 TO 25 STEP 3:F$(I,I+2)=E$:NEXT I
150     FOR I=1 TO 30 STEP 3:D$(I,I+2)=C$:NEXT I:PRINT :PRINT :
        PRINT :PRINT :PRINT
160     FOR I=1 TO 5:PRINT TAB$(1,7);D$:PRINT TAB$(1,7);D$:PRIN
        T TAB$(1,7);F$:NEXT I
170     PRINT TAB$(1,7);D$:PRINT TAB$(1,7);D$
180     R=2:C=0:POKE SC,128
190     PO=BE+(R*40)+C:POKE PO,YO
200     C1=26:R1=16:P1=BE+(R1*40)+C1:VE=PEEK(P1):POKE P1,MO
```

> Move your piece up, down, left and right

```
210     A=STICK(1):IF A=14 THEN GOSUB 370
220     IF A=13 THEN GOSUB 420
230     IF A=11 THEN GOSUB 470
```

```
240     IF A=7 THEN GOSUB 520
250     GOSUB 290
260     IF CN=45 THEN GOSUB 640:GOTO 10
270     POSITION 16,3:PRINT "SCORE";S1;
280     GOTO 210
290     IF SW<>AW THEN SW=SW+1:RETURN
300     SW=0
310     PC=P1:IF C1<C THEN C2=C1:C1=C1+1:P1=BE+(R1*40)+C1:IF PE
        EK(P1)=JL THEN C1=C2:P1=PC
320     IF C1>C THEN C2=C1:C1=C1-1:P1=BE+(R1*40)+C1:IF PEEK(P1)
        =JL THEN C1=C2:P1=PC
330     IF R1<R THEN R2=R1:R1=R1+1:P1=BE+(R1*40)+C1:IF PEEK(P1)
        =JL THEN R1=R2:P1=PC
340     IF R1>R THEN R2=R1:R1=R1-1:P1=BE+(R1*40)+C1:IF PEEK(P1)
        =JL THEN R1=R2:P1=PC
350     POKE PC,VE:VE=PEEK(P1):IF VE=YO THEN GOSUB 600:GOTO 10
360     POKE P1,MO:RETURN
370     IF R=0 THEN RETURN
380     T1=PO:R=R-1:PO=BE+(R*40)+C:IF PEEK(PO)=JL THEN PO=T1:R=
        R+1:RETURN
390     IF PEEK(PO)=13 THEN GOSUB 570
400     IF PEEK(PO)=DO THEN S1=S1+1:CN=CN+1
410     POKE T1,SP:POKE PO,YO:RETURN
420     IF R=16 THEN RETURN
430     T1=PO:R=R+1:PO=BE+(R*40)+C:IF PEEK(PO)=JL THEN PO=T1:R=
        R-1:RETURN
440     IF PEEK(PO)=DO THEN S1=S1+1:CN=CN+1
450     IF PEEK(PO)=MO THEN GOSUB 570
460     POKE T1,SP:POKE PO,YO:RETURN
470     IF C=0 THEN RETURN
480     T1=PO:C=C-1:PO=BE+(R*40)+C:IF PEEK(PO)=JL THEN C=C+1:PO
        =T1:RETURN
490     IF PEEK(PO)=DO THEN CN=CN+1:S1=S1+1
500     IF PEEK(PO)=MO THEN GOSUB 570
510     POKE T1,SP:POKE PO,YO:RETURN
520     IF C=28 THEN RETURN
530     T1=PO:C=C+1:PO=BE+(R*40)+C:IF PEEK(PO)=JL THEN C=C-1:PO
        =T1:RETURN
540     IF PEEK(PO)=DO THEN CN=CN+1:S1=S1+1
550     IF PEEK(PO)=MO THEN GOSUB 570
560     POKE T1,SP:POKE PO,YO:RETURN
```

> You ran into the hunter;
> you won the game

```
570     PRINT CHR$(125);:PRINT "YOU RAN STRAIGHT INTO THE HUNTE
        R!!!"
580     PRINT :PRINT :PRINT TAB$(1,13);"YOU ATE ";CN
590     PRINT :PRINT :GOSUB 680:GOTO 10
600     PRINT CHR$(125);:PRINT "   YOU WERE CAPTURED BY THE HUN
        TER!!!!!!!":PRINT :PRINT
610     PRINT TAB$(1,10);"YOU ATE ";CN;" POWER PILLS":PRINT :PR
        INT
620     GOSUB 680
630     RETURN
640     PRINT CHR$(125);
650     PRINT CHR$(125);TAB$(1,13);"CONGRATULATIONS"
```

```
660  PRINT :PRINT :PRINT :PRINT TAB$(1,5);"YOU HAVE COMPLETE
     D LEVEL:";TY
670  PRINT :PRINT :GOSUB 680:RETURN
680  PRINT TAB$(1,8);"PRESS FIRE BUTTON TO CONTINUE";:FOR I=
     1 TO 20:A=STRIG(1):NEXT I
690  A=STRIG(1):IF A=1 THEN 690
700  RETURN
710  PRINT CHR$(125);:PRINT TAB$(1,16);"HUNTER"
720  PRINT :PRINT :PRINT "MOVE AROUND THE SCREEN FOR AS LONG
      AS":PRINT
730  PRINT "POSSIBLE WITHOUT BEING DESTROYED BY THE":PRINT
740  PRINT "HUNTER. YOU GET POINTS FOR EATING THE":PRINT
750  PRINT "POWER PILLS. WHEN ALL ARE GONE YOU GET":PRINT
760  PRINT "ANOTHER GAME. MOVE YOUR MAN WITH THE":PRINT
770  PRINT "JOYSTICK":PRINT
780  PRINT :PRINT
830  GOSUB 680
840  RETURN
850  PRINT CHR$(125);:PRINT "DIFFICULTY LEVEL (1-4)";
860  INPUT A$:IF A$<"1" OR A$>"4" THEN 860
870  TY=VAL(A$):AW=4-TY:RETURN
```

ChexSum Tables

1 = 709	240 = 482	560 = 821
15 = 3374	250 = 259	570 = 2875
16 = 408	260 = 737	580 = 1435
20 = 356	270 = 1752	590 = 532
21 = 293	280 = 129	600 = 3226
22 = 2413	290 = 1035	610 = 2390
23 = 2783	300 = 292	620 = 247
24 = 2388	310 = 4542	630 = 58
25 = 1534	320 = 4063	640 = 356
26 = 2369	330 = 4067	650 = 2026
27 = 2160	340 = 4069	660 = 2739
30 = 136	350 = 1703	670 = 457
40 = 201	360 = 434	680 = 4071
50 = 356	370 = 305	690 = 1128
60 = 1229	380 = 3875	700 = 58
70 = 3146	390 = 744	710 = 1440
80 = 674	400 = 1689	720 = 2872
90 = 1448	410 = 821	730 = 2971
100 = 1419	420 = 391	740 = 2764
110 = 1825	430 = 3875	750 = 2776
120 = 2138	440 = 1689	760 = 2658
130 = 1225	450 = 784	770 = 772
140 = 1761	460 = 821	780 = 115
150 = 2347	470 = 306	830 = 247
160 = 2879	480 = 3887	840 = 58
170 = 1387	490 = 1689	850 = 1933
180 = 1028	500 = 784	860 = 949
190 = 1439	510 = 821	870 = 1250
200 = 2966	520 = 410	
210 = 1154	530 = 3887	
220 = 493	540 = 1689	TOTAL = 144648
230 = 571	550 = 784	

TAKEAWAY

```
All kneel the King will speak.
  SO VAGABOND YOU HAVE TRIED TO
STEAL MY GOLD.
VERY WELL ....NOW WE SHALL PLAY
A GAME.    THE OUTCOME OF WHICH
WILL DETERMINE YOU FATE....
IN THE CHEST BEFORE YOU ARE THE
100 GOLD PIECES THAT YOU DESIRE

WE SHALL TAKE TURNS AT REMOVING
FROM 1 TO 10 PIECES.
  IF YOU CAN TAKE THE LAST PIECE
THEN YOU WILL BE FREE TO LEAVE
WITH THE GOLD.

BUT... IF I TAKE THE LAST PIECE
I SHALL LEAVE WITH YOUR HEAD!

AS I AM THE KING I SHALL GO FIRST
I TAKE 1 LEAVING 99

How many will you take?
```

CLASSIFICATION: Logic

You and the computer take turns at removing gold pieces from a chest. The player with no pieces to remove loses his head. The game is self prompting. Note: The game can't lose. Use this to show your friends how 'smart' your computer is.

PROGRAMMING SUGGESTIONS

Music for introduction page. More ancient sounding insults etc.

Program Variables

CHEAT	Counts number of times player attempts to cheat
FLAG	Flag
GOLD	Number of gold pieces remaining
R	Local
R$	Local string
TAKE	Number of pieces taken by player
X,Y,Z	Used in z=x mod y routine

Program Structure

10	Initialize the game
20 - 130	Introductory text
1000 - 1060	Player's turn
1070 - 1130	Machine's turn
3000 - 3040	X mod Y routine
5000 - 5050	Cheat routine
6000 - 7040	Game end
8000	You have attempted to cheat three times
9000 - 9060	Insult routine

Listing

Initialize the game

```
10    ? CHR$(125)::DIM R$(20):CHEAT=0:FLAG=0
20    ? "All kneel the King will speak.":?
30    ? "  SO VAGABOND YOU HAVE TRIED TO"
40    ? "STEAL MY GOLD."
50    ? :? "VERY WELL.....NOW WE SHALL PLAY"
60    ? "A GAME.    THE OUTCOME OF WHICH"
70    ? "WILL DETERMINE YOU FATE...."
80    ? "IN THE CHEST BEFORE YOU ARE THE":? "100 GOLD PIECES THAT YOU DESIRE"
90    ? :? "WE SHALL TAKE TURNS AT REMOVING"
100   ? "FROM 1 TO 10 PIECES."
110   ? " IF YOU CAN TAKE THE LAST PIECE":? "THEN YOU WILL BE FREE TO LEAVE"
120   ? "WITH THE GOLD.":? :? "BUT.. IF I TAKE THE LAST PIECE":? "I SHALL LEAVE WITH YOUR HEAD!"
130   ? :? "AS I AM THE KING I SHALL GO FIRST":? "I TAKE 1 LEAVING 99"
```

Player turn

```
1000  GOLD=99
1020  IF CHEAT=3 THEN 8000
1025  GOSUB 9000:? :? "How many will you take";:INPUT TAKE:?
1030  IF TAKE>GOLD THEN GOSUB 5000:GOTO 1020
1040  IF TAKE>10 THEN GOSUB 5000:GOTO 1020
1050  GOLD=GOLD-TAKE
1060  ? "You have taken ";TAKE;" leaving ";GOLD:?
1070  ? "We will take ";
1080  X=GOLD:Y=11:GOSUB 3000
1090  ? Z
1100  GOLD=GOLD-Z
1110  ? "Which leaves ";GOLD
1120  IF GOLD=0 THEN 6000
1130  ? :? :GOTO 1020
```

X mod Y routine

```
3000  Z=X/Y
3010  Z=Z-INT(Z)
3020  Z=Z+1/(Y*10)
3030  Z=INT(Z*Y)
3040  RETURN
```

Cheat routine

```
5000  CHEAT=CHEAT+1:? :? :? :R=INT(RND(0)*4):ON R GOTO 5020,5
      030,5040,5050
5010  ? "THOU CHEAT... TAKE CARE!!!":RETURN
5020  ? "BE THOU BLIND OR FOOLISH":RETURN
5030  ? "HAVE THY WITS FLED THEE":RETURN
5040  ? "THOU CONSPIRE TO DEFRAUD ME..":? "THEE SON OF A CEPH
      ALOPOD.":RETURN
5050  ? "GUARD THY HONOUR THOU VARLET.":RETURN
```

Game end

```
6000  ? :? :? "WHICH MEANS THAT I HAVE WON..."
6010  ? :? :? "OFF WITH HIS HEAD!!!!"
6020  ? "Are there any other theives"
6030  ? "wishing to play the Kings game":? :? "Y OR N":INPUT
      R$
6040  IF R$="N" OR R$="n" THEN 7000
6050  IF R$="Y" OR R$="y" THEN RUN
6060  GOSUB 5030:? :GOTO 6020
```

Final message

```
7000  ? :? :? "It is well that you have declined":? "to play
      the King."
7010  ? "As a palace guard I will tell you":? "that the King
      NEVER loses."
7020  ? :? "The King can t lose....."
7030  ? :? :? "FAREWELL...."
7040  END
```

You have attempted to cheat three times

```
8000  ? :? :? "YOU HAVE ANGERED ME WITH YOUR":? "FOOLISH ATTE
      MPTS TO CHEAT!!":? :? :GOTO 6010
```

Insult routine

```
9000  IF FLAG=0 THEN FLAG=1:RETURN
9010  X=INT(RND(0)*5):ON X GOTO 9030,9040,9050,9060
9020  ? "Thy doom draws closer.":RETURN
9030  ? "Hast thy will been drawn?":RETURN
```

```
9040  ? "Choose,thou noxious vermin.":RETURN
9050  ? "Thee suffer nympholepsy.":RETURN
9060  ? "Halt thy procrastination whelp.":RETURN
```

ChexSum Tables

```
  10 = 1396         1080 = 944         6040 = 868
  20 = 2908         1090 = 197         6050 = 756
  30 = 2156         1100 = 556         6060 = 580
  40 = 1038         1110 = 1445        7000 = 5031
  50 = 2270         1120 = 410         7010 = 5479
  60 = 2042         1130 = 307         7020 = 2100
  70 = 1906         3000 = 562         7030 = 1022
  80 = 4403         3010 = 746         7040 = 43
  90 = 2367         3020 = 897         8000 = 4890
 100 = 1329         3030 = 743         9000 = 655
 110 = 4314         3040 = 58          9010 = 2248
 120 = 5331         5000 = 2750        9020 = 2263
 130 = 3679         5010 = 1782        9030 = 2516
1000 = 483          5020 = 1829        9040 = 2855
1020 = 507          5030 = 1759        9050 = 2567
1025 = 2885         5040 = 4023        9060 = 3258
1030 = 728          5050 = 2249
1040 = 703          6000 = 2235
1050 = 553          6010 = 1527        TOTAL = 113564
1060 = 2714         6020 = 2682
1070 = 1256         6030 = 3764
```

SORTGAME

CLASSIFICATION: Strategy

Object of game is to unscramble the board in the smallest possible number of moves. To make a move press the key that corresponds to the letter on the board that you wish to move.

PROGRAMMING SUGGESTIONS

The scramble routine could be sped up considerably by resorting to machine language.

Program Variables

A	Local
BOARD()	Holds board
CHR	Screen code for letters
DL	Local
M	Local
M1	Local
M2	Local
MOVES	Number of times board altered
MV	Local
SLOC	Address of video RAM
TOTAL	Count of moves made
VALID	Flags valid move
WHAT	Holds what to do from menu
X1	Local
Y	Local
Y1	Local
Z	Local

Program Structure

10	Jump to initialize routine
90	Select graphics mode
100 - 300	Main loop
1000 - 1050	End game
5000 - 5110	Draw board in GR.0
6000 - 6110	Draw board in GR.2
7000 - 7080	Make a move
20000 - 22160	Initialize the system

Listing

```
10      OPEN #1,4,0,"K:":GOTO 20000
```

> Select graphics mode

```
90      GRAPHICS 2
```

> Main loop

```
100     GOSUB 6000
110     ? CHR$(125)
111     SETCOLOR 4,3,3
120     ? "PRESS MOVE";
130     GET #1,A
140     M=A-64
150     IF M<1 OR M>15 THEN 100
160     GOSUB 7000
180     IF VALID THEN TOTAL=TOTAL+1
200     Z=0:FOR X=1 TO 4:FOR Y=1 TO 4:IF BOARD(X,Y)<>Z THEN X=4
        :Y=4
210     Z=Z+1:NEXT Y:NEXT X
220     IF Z=16 THEN 1000
300     GOTO 100
```

> End game

```
1000    GRAPHICS 0:GOSUB 5000
1010    POSITION 4,10:? "COMPLETED IN ";TOTAL;" MOVES":IF MOVES
        =TOTAL THEN ? "PERFECT!"
1020    ? :? :? "PRESS <RETURN> FOR ANOTHER GAME"
1030    GET #1,A
1040    IF A<>155 THEN 1030
1050    RUN
```

> Draw board in GR.0

```
5000    ? CHR$(125)
5010    FOR X=1 TO 4
5060    FOR Y=1 TO 4
5070    Z=BOARD(X,Y):IF Z=0 THEN ? "  ";
5080    IF Z THEN ? CHR$(64+Z);" ";
5090    NEXT Y:?
5100    NEXT X
5110    RETURN
```

Draw board in GR.2

```
6000 DL=PEEK(560)+PEEK(561)*256:SLOC=PEEK(DL+4)+PEEK(DL+5)*2
     56
6010 FOR X=1 TO 4
6060 FOR Y=1 TO 4
6070 Z=BOARD(X,Y):IF Z=0 THEN CHR=0
6080 IF Z THEN CHR=Z+32+(INT(Z/4)*64)
6090 POKE X*20+Y+SLOC+7+20,CHR
6100 NEXT Y:NEXT X
6110 RETURN
```

Make a move

```
7000 VALID=1
7010 FOR X=1 TO 4:FOR Y=1 TO 4:IF BOARD(X,Y)=M THEN X1=X:Y1=
     Y
7020 NEXT Y:NEXT X
7040 IF BOARD(X1-1,Y1)=0 THEN BOARD(X1-1,Y1)=M:BOARD(X1,Y1)=
     0:RETURN
7050 IF BOARD(X1+1,Y1)=0 THEN BOARD(X1+1,Y1)=M:BOARD(X1,Y1)=
     0:RETURN
7060 IF BOARD(X1,Y1+1)=0 THEN BOARD(X1,Y1+1)=M:BOARD(X1,Y1)=
     0:RETURN
7070 IF BOARD(X1,Y1-1)=0 THEN BOARD(X1,Y1-1)=M:BOARD(X1,Y1)=
     0:RETURN
7080 VALID=0:RETURN
```

Initialize the system

```
20000 DIM BOARD(5,5):FOR X=0 TO 5:FOR Y=0 TO 5:BOARD(X,Y)=99:
      NEXT Y:NEXT X
20010 Z=0:FOR X=1 TO 4:FOR Y=1 TO 4
20020 BOARD(X,Y)=Z:Z=Z+1:NEXT Y:NEXT X
21000 GRAPHICS 0:? CHR$(125):? :? :? "SELECT":? :? :? "  1 = 
      NEW BOARD":? :? "  2 = SCRAMBLE DISPLAY":?
21010 ? "  3 = SCRAMBLE":? :INPUT WHAT:IF WHAT<1 OR WHAT>3 TH
      EN 21000
22000 TOTAL=0:IF WHAT=1 THEN 90
22010 ? :? "HOW MANY MOVES TO SCRAMBLE";:INPUT MOVES
22020 GRAPHICS 2
22100 M1=0:M2=0:FOR MV=1 TO MOVES
22110 M=INT(RND(0)*15)+1:IF M=M1 OR M=M2 THEN 22110
22120 GOSUB 7000:IF VALID=0 THEN 22110
22130 M2=M1:M1=M
22140 IF WHAT=2 THEN GOSUB 6000
22150 NEXT MV
22160 GOTO 90
```

ChexSum Tables

```
  10 = 609          5000 = 343         7060 = 2659
  90 = 145          5010 = 394         7070 = 2661
 100 = 209          5060 = 395         7080 = 339
 110 = 343          5070 = 1251       20000 = 2761
 111 = 350          5080 = 856        20010 = 1142
 120 = 848          5090 = 235        20020 = 1735
 130 = 316          5100 = 164        21000 = 4317
 140 = 594          5110 = 58         21010 = 1955
 150 = 678          6000 = 2632       22000 = 832
 160 = 225          6010 = 394        22010 = 2239
 180 = 684          6060 = 395        22020 = 145
 200 = 2803         6070 = 1365       22100 = 1081
 210 = 872          6080 = 1540       22110 = 1765
 220 = 417          6090 = 1104       22120 = 621
 300 = 112          6100 = 338        22130 = 814
1000 = 293          6110 = 58         22140 = 524
1010 = 3000         7000 = 330        22150 = 176
1020 = 2451         7010 = 2555       22160 = 254
1030 = 316          7020 = 338
1040 = 522          7040 = 2661
1050 = 59           7050 = 2659       TOTAL = 61931
```

SLEFT

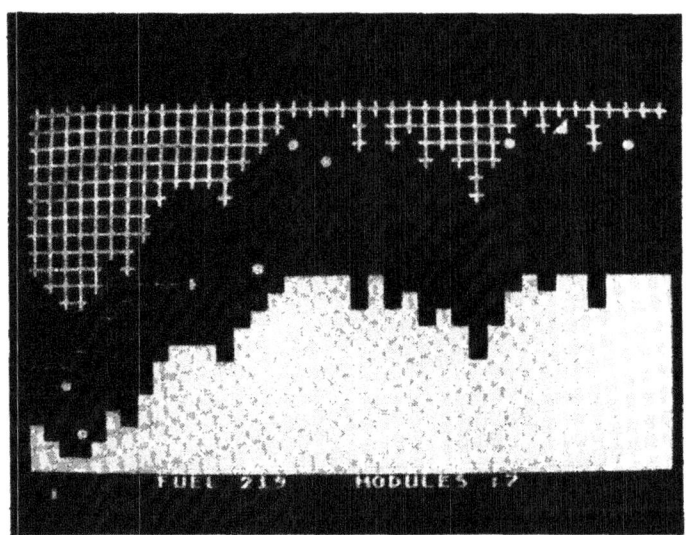

CLASSIFICATION: Evasion

The object of the game is to collect as many modules as possible. You also need to avoid mines, the roof and floor of the cave, and running out of fuel. Hitting a mine (solid circle) loses one man. Hitting a fuel container (*) adds 50 to your fuel. Modules are solid triangles. Joystick 1 controls movement.

PROGRAMMING SUGGESTIONS

Add enemy missiles to the game to make it more difficult. Make the missiles heat seeking and give the player some way of destroying them.

Program Variables

A	Used to set up machine code scroll routine
DL	Used to calculate starting address of video RAM
FLAG	Flag for sound effects
FLAG2	As above
FUEL	Remaining fuel
MEN	Number of men
OLDP	Old position of ship
P	Current position of ship
Q	Screen code of whatever the ship hits
R	=53770 Where to peek for a random number 0 - 255
SCREEN	Address of start of video RAM
SIZE	Height of cave
T	Local variable, many uses
U	What to put on screen
X$	Local
XZ	Address of top right of screen
Y	Position of top of cave
YP	Vertical position of ship
Z	Local, many uses

Program Structure

10	Jump to initialize routine
100 - 250	Main loop
1000 - 1080	Setup machine language routine
2000 - 2070	Hit something
2300 - 2330	Game over
3000 - 3010	Collect Fuel
4000 - 4010	Collect module
5000 - 5040	Out of fuel
8000 - 8010	Display number of men left
20000 - 21080	Initialization routine

Listing

```
10      SETCOLOR 1,10,10:SETCOLOR 2,10,0:? CHR$(125):GOTO 20000
```

Main loop

```
100     POKE 205,Y:POKE 206,SIZE:IF FLAG THEN SOUND 1,20,6,FLAG
        :FLAG=FLAG-1
101     POSITION 13,22:? FUEL;" ▲";:FUEL=FUEL-1:IF  NOT FUEL THE
        N 5000
102     IF FLAG2 THEN FLAG2=FLAG2-2:SOUND 0,50,10,FLAG2
110     Z=INT(RND(0)*5)-2:Y=Y+Z:IF Y<1 THEN Y=1
121     T=0:IF PEEK(R)>191 THEN T=Y*40+INT(RND(0)*SIZE)*40+XZ:P
        OKE T,84
123     U=10:IF PEEK(R)>127 THEN U=72
124     IF T AND PEEK(R)>191 THEN POKE T,U
130     IF Y+SIZE>21 THEN Y=21-SIZE
220     Z=USR(20527):Z=USR(20480)
225     Z=STICK(0):IF Z=14 AND YP THEN YP=YP-1
226     IF Z=13 AND YP<22 THEN YP=YP+1
230     OLDP=P:P=SCREEN+YP*40+10:POKE OLDP-1,13:Q=PEEK(P):IF Q
        THEN 2000
250     POKE P,127:GOTO 100
```

Setup machine language routine

```
1000    RESTORE 1010:FOR T=20480 TO 20613:READ A:POKE T,A:NEXT
        T:RETURN
1010    DATA 104,169,64,133,203,169,156,133,204,162,22,160,0,20
        0,177,203,136,145,203,200
1020    DATA 152,201,40,208,234,136,169,0,145,203,165,203,24,10
        5,40,133,203,165,204,105
1030    DATA 0,133,204,202,208,221,96
1040    DATA 104,169,103,133,203,169,156,133,204,165,205,170,16
        0,0,169, 83,145,203,24,165
1050    DATA 203,105,40,133,203,165,204,105,0,133,204,202,208,2
        36,165,206,170,24,165,203
1060    DATA 105,40,133,203,165,204,105,0,133,204,202,208,240,1
        65,205,24,101,206,133,207
1070    DATA 56,169,22,229,207,170,169,128,145,203,24,165,203,1
        05,40,133,203,165,204,105
1080    DATA 0,133,204,202,208,236,96
```

Hit something

```
2000    IF Q=10 THEN 3000
2010    IF Q=72 THEN 4000
2020    FOR T=15 TO 0 STEP -0.25
```

```
2030    POKE P,T:SOUND 1,50,0,T
2040    NEXT T
2050    MEN=MEN-1
2060    IF MEN=0 THEN 2300
2070    GOTO 21000
2300    ? CHR$(125):? :? :? " GAME OVER "
2310    SOUND 0,0,0,0:SOUND 1,0,0,0:? :? :? "   YOU COLLECTED "
        ;MODULES;" MODULES"
2320    ? :? :? "PRESS <RETURN> FOR ANOTHER GAME";:INPUT X$
2330    RUN
```

Collect Fuel

```
3000    SOUND 1,50,6,15:FUEL=FUEL+50:FLAG=15
3010    GOTO 100
```

Collect module

```
4000    MODULES=MODULES+1:POSITION 20,22:? "MODULES :";MODULES;
4010    FLAG2=14:GOTO 100
```

Out of fuel

```
5000    ? CHR$(125)
5010    POSITION 10,11:? " OUT OF FUEL "
5020    FOR T=255 TO 0 STEP -1
5030    SOUND 1,T,12,8:NEXT T
5040    SOUND 1,0,0,0:GOTO 2300
```

Display number of men left

```
8000    POSITION 1,23:? "   ";
8010    FOR T=1 TO MEN:POKE SCREEN+920+T,127:NEXT T:RETURN
```

Initialization routine

```
20000   GOSUB 1000:DIM X$(9):POKE 752,255
20010   DL=PEEK(560)+PEEK(561)*256
20020   SCREEN=PEEK(DL+4)+256*PEEK(DL+5)
20060   MODULES=0
20070   MEN=3
21000   Y=1:SIZE=9:POKE 205,Y:POKE 206,SIZE:FUEL=300:YP=4
21001   P=SCREEN+YP*40+10:OLDP=P
21010   FOR T=1 TO 40
21020   Z=USR(20527):Z=USR(20480)
```

```
21030 NEXT T
21040 POSITION 8,22:? "FUEL▲:";
21050 GOSUB 8000
21060 XZ=SCREEN+39
21070 R=53770
21080 GOTO 100
```

ChexSum Tables

```
   10 = 1319        1070 = 3852       5030 = 721
  100 = 1995        1080 = 1337       5040 = 438
  101 = 1620        2000 = 460        8000 = 502
  102 = 1293        2010 = 574        8010 = 1478
  110 = 2224        2020 = 542       20000 = 985
  121 = 2978        2030 = 900       20010 = 1220
  123 = 1386        2040 = 166       20020 = 1400
  124 = 1159        2050 = 540       20060 = 287
  130 = 1062        2060 = 369       20070 = 353
  220 = 1225        2070 = 130       21000 = 2204
  225 = 1558        2300 = 1322      21001 = 1352
  226 = 1203        2310 = 2827      21010 = 456
  230 = 2871        2320 = 2698      21020 = 1225
  250 = 472         2330 = 59        21030 = 166
 1000 = 1710        3000 = 1608      21040 = 808
 1010 = 3833        3010 = 112       21050 = 241
 1020 = 3777        4000 = 1838      21060 = 584
 1030 = 1331        4010 = 494       21070 = 515
 1040 = 3884        5000 = 343       21080 = 112
 1050 = 3820        5010 = 2890
 1060 = 3810        5020 = 574      TOTAL = 83212
```

OXO

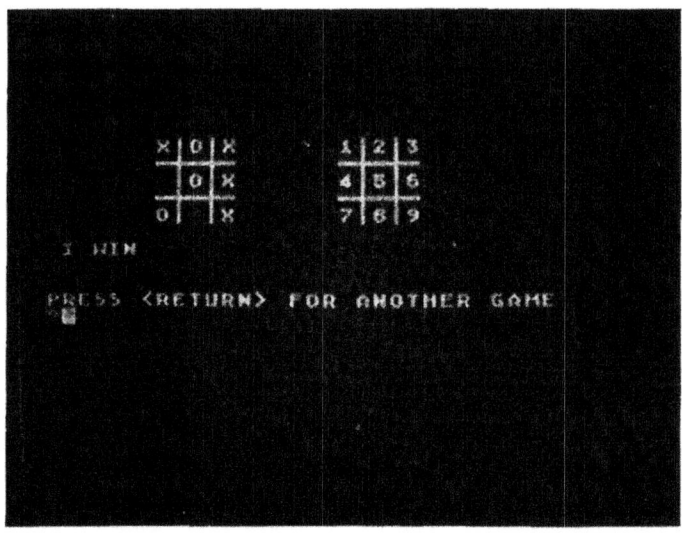

CLASSIFICATION: Strategy

A standard noughts and crosses game. You play the computer. This program is self prompting.

PROGRAMMING SUGGESTIONS

Use a cursor to input moves (see OTHELLO).

Program Variables

A	Local
B	Local
C	Local
EVAL	1,-1 or 0 Evaluation win, loose or draw
FULL	=1 if no space on board
INDEX	Local, several uses
LOOP	Loop counter
MNUM	Local in evaluation routine
MOVE	Flags who's turn it is
MOVE( )	Holds intermediate results
PM	Holds players move number
Q	Flag as in EVAL
R	Used if machine moves first

```
R$                  Local
SCORE()             Score table
T                   Local, many uses
W                   Local to print board routine
WORKBOARD()         Copy of PLAYBOARD()
X                   Local
X$                  Local
Z                   Local
```

Program Structure

```
   10 -      10   Jump to initialization
 5000 -    5190   Draw Board
 6000 -    6230   Evaluate proposed move
 7000 -    7030   Check if board full
 8000 -    8010   Set scoring table
10000 -   10050   Evaluate subroutine
```

Listing

```
10      GOTO 20000
```

Get & do move

```
1000    ? CHR$(125):GOSUB 5000:GOSUB 7000:IF FULL=1 OR EVAL<>0
        THEN 12000
1010    POSITION 9,22:IF MOVE=1 THEN ? "MY MOVE":GOTO 2000
1020    ? "WHERE TO?";:INPUT PM
1030    IF PM<1 OR PM>9 THEN ? CHR$(125):GOSUB 5000:GOTO 1000
1040    IF PLAYBOARD(PM)<>0 THEN ? "INVALID MOVE":FOR PM=1 TO 1
        000:NEXT PM:GOTO 1000
1050    PLAYBOARD(PM)=-1:MOVE=-MOVE:GOSUB 5000
1060    FOR T=1 TO 9:WORKBOARD(T)=PLAYBOARD(T):NEXT T
1070    GOSUB 7000
1080    IF EVAL<>0 OR FULL<>0 THEN 12000
```

Machines move

```
2000    INDEX=0:FOR T=0 TO 9:MOVE(T)=99:SCORE(T)=99:NEXT T
2001    MOVE=-MOVE
2010    GOSUB 7000:IF FULL THEN 9000
2100    FOR LOOP=1 TO 9
2110    IF PLAYBOARD(LOOP)<>0 THEN 3000
2120    FOR T=1 TO 9:WORKBOARD(T)=PLAYBOARD(T):NEXT T
2130    WORKBOARD(LOOP)=1:GOSUB 6000
2140    MOVE(INDEX)=LOOP:SCORE(INDEX)=EVAL
2150    INDEX=INDEX+1
3000    NEXT LOOP
```

Aggressive move

```
4000    Q=0:MNUM=0:FOR X=0 TO 9
4010    IF SCORE(X)=1 THEN MNUM=MOVE(X):Q=1
4020    NEXT X
4030    IF Q THEN PLAYBOARD(MNUM)=1:GOTO 1000
```

Defensive move

```
4100    Q=0:MNUM=0:FOR X=0 TO 9
4110    IF SCORE(X)=0 THEN MNUM=MOVE(X):Q=1
4120    NEXT X
4130    IF Q<>0 THEN PLAYBOARD(MNUM)=1:GOTO 1000
```

```
4200  Q=0:MNUM=0:FOR X=0 TO 9
4210  IF SCORE(X)=-1 THEN MNUM=MOVE(X):Q=1
4220  NEXT X
4230  IF Q<>0 THEN PLAYBOARD(MNUM)=1:GOTO 1000
```

> Error if here

```
4240  STOP
```

> Draw Board

```
5000  POSITION 9,4
5010  W=0:FOR X=1 TO 3:GOSUB 5100
5011  W=W+1:IF W<3 THEN ? "|";
5012  NEXT X
5013  POSITION 9,5:? "—+—+—"
5020  POSITION 9,6
5030  W=0:FOR X=4 TO 6:GOSUB 5100
5031  W=W+1:IF W<3 THEN ? "|";
5032  NEXT X
5033  POSITION 9,7:? "—+—+—"
5040  POSITION 9,8
5050  W=0:FOR X=7 TO 9:GOSUB 5100
5051  W=W+1:IF W<3 THEN ? "|";
5052  NEXT X
5060  GOTO 5140
5100  Z=PLAYBOARD(X):IF Z=0 THEN ? "▲";
5110  IF Z=-1 THEN ? "O";
5120  IF Z=1 THEN ? "X";
5130  RETURN
5140  POSITION 20,4:? "1|2|3";
5150  POSITION 20,5:? "—+—+—";
5160  POSITION 20,6:? "4|5|6";
5170  POSITION 20,7:? "—+—+—";
5180  POSITION 20,8:? "7|8|9";
5190  RETURN
```

> Evaluate proposed move

```
6000  A=WORKBOARD(7):B=WORKBOARD(5):C=WORKBOARD(3)
6010  IF A=1 AND B=1 AND C=1 THEN EVAL=1:RETURN
6020  IF A=-1 AND B=-1 AND C=0 THEN EVAL=-1:RETURN
6021  IF A=-1 AND B=0 AND C=-1 THEN EVAL=-1:RETURN
6023  IF A=0 AND B=-1 AND C=-1 THEN EVAL=-1:RETURN
6030  A=WORKBOARD(1):C=WORKBOARD(9)
6040  IF A=1 AND B=1 AND C=1 THEN EVAL=1:RETURN
6050  IF A=-1 AND B=-1 AND C=0 THEN EVAL=-1:RETURN
6051  IF A=-1 AND B=0 AND C=-1 THEN EVAL=-1:RETURN
6052  IF A=0 AND B=-1 AND C=-1 THEN EVAL=-1:RETURN
```

```
                    ┌─────────────────────────────────┐
                    │   Evaluate horizontal lines     │
                    └─────────────────────────────────┘

6120    Q=0:FOR T=1 TO 7 STEP 3:A=WORKBOARD(T):B=WORKBOARD(T+1)
        :C=WORKBOARD(T+2)
6130    IF A=1 AND B=1 AND C=1 THEN Q=1:T=99:GOTO 6150
6140    IF A=-1 AND B=-1 AND C=0 THEN Q=-1
6141    IF A=-1 AND B=0 AND C=-1 THEN Q=-1
6142    IF A=0 AND B=-1 AND C=-1 THEN Q=-1
6150    NEXT T:IF Q<>0 THEN EVAL=Q:RETURN

                    ┌─────────────────────────────────┐
                    │    Evaluate vertical lines      │
                    └─────────────────────────────────┘

6180    FOR T=1 TO 3:A=WORKBOARD(T):B=WORKBOARD(T+3):C=WORKBOAR
        D(T+6)
6190    IF A=1 AND B=1 AND C=1 THEN Q=1:T=99:GOTO 6210
6200    IF A=-1 AND B=-1 AND C=0 THEN Q=-1
6201    IF A=-1 AND B=0 AND C=-1 THEN Q=-1
6202    IF A=0 AND B=-1 AND C=-1 THEN Q=-1
6210    NEXT T
6230    EVAL=Q:RETURN

                    ┌─────────────────────────────────┐
                    │     Check if board full         │
                    └─────────────────────────────────┘

7000    FULL=1:FOR T=1 TO 9:WORKBOARD(T)=PLAYBOARD(T):IF PLAYBO
        ARD(T)=0 THEN FULL=0
7010    NEXT T
7020    GOSUB 10000
7030    RETURN

                    ┌─────────────────────────────────┐
                    │      Set scoring table          │
                    └─────────────────────────────────┘

8000    FOR T=0 TO 9:? MOVE(T),SCORE(T):NEXT T

                    ┌─────────────────────────────────┐
                    │      Evaluate subroutine        │
                    └─────────────────────────────────┘

9000    POSITION 9,1:? " GAME OVER  ":STOP
10000   EVAL=0:A=WORKBOARD(7):B=WORKBOARD(5):C=WORKBOARD(3)
10010   IF A=1 AND B=1 AND C=1 THEN EVAL=1:RETURN
10020   IF A=-1 AND B=-1 AND C=-1 THEN EVAL=-1:RETURN
10030   A=WORKBOARD(1):C=WORKBOARD(9)
10040   IF A=1 AND B=1 AND C=1 THEN EVAL=1:RETURN
10050   IF A=-1 AND B=-1 AND C=-1 THEN EVAL=-1:RETURN
```

Evaluate diagonal lines

```
10120 Q=0:FOR T=1 TO 7 STEP 3:A=WORKBOARD(T):B=WORKBOARD(T+1)
      :C=WORKBOARD(T+2)
10130 IF A=1 AND B=1 AND C=1 THEN Q=1
10140 IF A=-1 AND B=-1 AND C=-1 THEN Q=-1
10150 NEXT T:IF Q<>0 THEN EVAL=Q:RETURN
```

Win, lose or draw

```
10200 FOR T=1 TO 3:A=WORKBOARD(T):B=WORKBOARD(T+3):C=WORKBOAR
      D(T+6)
10210 IF A=1 AND B=1 AND C=1 THEN Q=1:T=99:GOTO 6210
10220 IF A=-1 AND B=-1 AND C=-1 THEN Q=-1
10230 NEXT T
10240 EVAL=Q:RETURN
10250 REM G.STRETTON 85
12000 ? :? :IF EVAL=-1 THEN ? "YOU WIN":GOTO 12030
12010 IF EVAL=1 THEN ? " I WIN":GOTO 12030
12020 IF FULL=1 THEN ? " A DRAW"
12030 ? :? :? "PRESS <RETURN> FOR ANOTHER GAME"
12040 INPUT X$
12050 RUN
```

Initialize

```
20000 DIM WORKBOARD(9),PLAYBOARD(9),R$(10),SCORE(9),MOVE(9),X
      $(9)
20010 MOVE=-1
20020 ? CHR$(125)
20030 DL=PEEK(560)+PEEK(561)*256
20100 FOR INDEX=0 TO 9:PLAYBOARD(INDEX)=0:NEXT INDEX
21000 ? "WILL YOU MOVE FIRST (Y/N)";:INPUT R$
21010 IF R$="Y" OR R$="y" THEN 1000
21020 IF R$<>"N" AND R$<>"n" THEN ? :? "SORRY":? :GOTO 21000
21030 R=INT(RND(0)*5)*2+1
21040 PLAYBOARD(R)=1
21050 GOTO 1000
```

ChexSum Tables

10 = 114	5032 = 179	7010 = 166
1000 = 1523	5033 = 460	7020 = 115
1010 = 1434	5040 = 258	7030 = 58
1020 = 927	5050 = 974	8000 = 1409
1030 = 1387	5051 = 1117	9000 = 1201
1040 = 2330	5052 = 179	10000 = 2192
1050 = 1335	5060 = 256	10010 = 1403
1060 = 1509	5100 = 1075	10020 = 1627
1070 = 225	5110 = 552	10030 = 1225
1080 = 571	5120 = 506	10040 = 1403
2000 = 2451	5130 = 58	10050 = 1627
2001 = 451	5140 = 808	10120 = 3209
2010 = 663	5150 = 503	10130 = 1306
2100 = 411	5160 = 819	10140 = 1526
2110 = 612	5170 = 505	10150 = 920
2120 = 1509	5180 = 830	10200 = 2722
2130 = 821	5190 = 58	10210 = 2142
2140 = 1314	6000 = 1868	10220 = 1526
2150 = 521	6010 = 1403	10230 = 166
3000 = 176	6020 = 1506	10240 = 472
4000 = 982	6021 = 1506	12000 = 1365
4010 = 1608	6023 = 1506	12010 = 995
4020 = 179	6030 = 1225	12020 = 825
4030 = 946	6040 = 1403	12030 = 2451
4100 = 982	6050 = 1506	12040 = 178
4110 = 1543	6051 = 1506	12050 = 59
4120 = 179	6052 = 1506	20000 = 2148
4130 = 1006	6120 = 3209	20010 = 392
4200 = 982	6130 = 2205	20020 = 343
4210 = 1664	6140 = 1406	20030 = 1222
4220 = 179	6141 = 1406	20100 = 1109
4230 = 1006	6142 = 1406	21000 = 2029
4240 = 60	6150 = 920	21010 = 848
5000 = 254	6180 = 2722	21020 = 1573
5010 = 962	6190 = 2142	21030 = 999
5011 = 1117	6200 = 1406	21040 = 597
5012 = 179	6201 = 1406	21050 = 127
5013 = 458	6202 = 1406	
5020 = 256	6210 = 166	TOTAL = 127479
5030 = 968	6230 = 472	
5031 = 1117	7000 = 2549	

PINGPONG

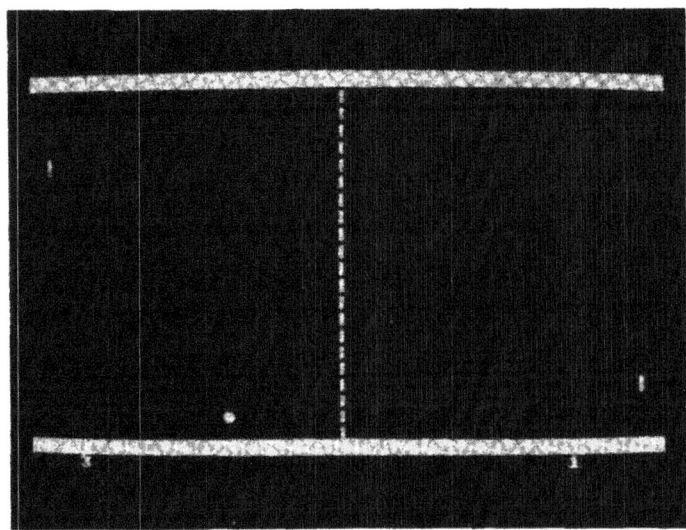

CLASSIFICATION: Reflex

This is a two player game, the objective being to keep the ball going as long as possible. Joysticks move the bats up and down. There is a practice mode in which you can play the ball against the wall. Pressing the fire button on the joystick serves the ball.

PROGRAMMING SUGGESTIONS

Ball's rebound could be made dependant on bat's direction at time of hit. Size of bats could be varied to make game harder/easier.

Program Variables

BALL	Screen code for ball
BALLH	Ball's horizontal position
BALLV	Ball's vertical position
BAT1	Player 1's bat position
BAT2	Player 2's bat position
DIRH	Ball's horizontal direction 1 or −1
DIRV	Ball's vertical direction 1 or −1
OBAT1	Bat 1's old position
OBAT2	Bat 2's old position

OLDBALLH	Ball's old horizontal position
OLDBALLV	Ball's old vertical position
QZ	Constant in joystick routine
SCORE1	Player 2's score
SCREEN	Address of start of screen
SERVE	Who serves 1 or 2
T	Local variable
WALL$	Holds graphics for wall
X$	Local variable
Z	Local variable

Program Structure

10		Jump to initialization
20 -	30	Put bats onto the screen
100 -	250	Main loop
4000 -	4030	Game end
5000 -	5030	Draw court
20000 -	23000	Intialization routine

Listing

```
10      POKE 752,1:GOTO 20000
```

Put bats onto the screen

```
20      POKE SCREEN+40*OBAT1+2,0:POKE SCREEN+40*BAT1+2,124:IF P
        RACT THEN RETURN
30      POKE SCREEN+40*OBAT2+38,0:POKE SCREEN+40*BAT2+38,124:RE
        TURN
```

Main loop

```
100     OBAT1=BAT1:OBAT2=BAT2:Z=STICK(0)/2:IF Z=QZ THEN 140
110     IF BAT1>1 AND Z=INT(Z) THEN BAT1=BAT1-1
120     IF BAT1<21 AND Z<>INT(Z) THEN BAT1=BAT1+1
140     Z=STICK(1)/2:IF Z=QZ THEN 160
142     IF BAT2>1 AND Z=INT(Z) THEN BAT2=BAT2-1
150     IF BAT2<21 AND Z<>INT(Z) THEN BAT2=BAT2+1
160     IF BALLH=37 AND PRACT THEN DIRH=-1:DIRV=INT(RND(0)*3)-1
        :SOUND 0,20,10,9
170     GOSUB 20:OLDBALLH=BALLH:OLDBALLV=BALLV:BALLH=BALLH+DIRH
        :IF BALLH<2 OR BALLH>38 THEN GOTO 900
190     SOUND 0,0,0,0:Z=DIRV+BALLV:IF Z<1 THEN DIRV=1:SOUND 0,1
        21,10,9
200     IF Z>21 THEN DIRV=-1:SOUND 0,100,10,9
210     BALLV=BALLV+DIRV:Z=BALLH+40*BALLV+SCREEN:IF PEEK(Z)=124
         THEN DIRH=-DIRH:DIRV=INT(RND(0)*3)-1:SOUND 0,30,10,9
240     POKE Z,BALL:IF OLDBALLH<>20 THEN POKE OLDBALLH+40*OLDBA
        LLV+SCREEN,0:GOTO 100
250     POKE OLDBALLH+40*OLDBALLV+SCREEN,26:GOTO 100
```

Adjust score and serve

```
900     SERVE=1:IF BALLH<2 THEN SERVE=2
1000    IF SERVE=1 THEN SCORE1=SCORE1+1
1010    IF SERVE=2 THEN SCORE2=SCORE2+1
1020    IF SCORE1=15 OR SCORE2=15 THEN 4000
1030    IF PRACT THEN SERVE=1
2000    GOSUB 5000:BALLV=10:SOUND 0,0,0,0
2010    POSITION 4,23:? SCORE1;:POSITION 34,23:? SCORE2;
2020    IF SERVE=1 THEN BALLH=3:DIRH=1
2030    IF SERVE=2 THEN BALLH=37:DIRH=-1
2035    BAT1=10:BAT2=10:OBAT1=BAT1:OBAT2=BAT2:GOSUB 20
2040    POKE SCREEN+40*BALLV+BALLH,BALL
2050    IF SERVE=1 AND STRIG(0) THEN 2050
2060    IF SERVE=2 AND STRIG(1) THEN 2060
```

```
2070    DIRV=INT(RND(0)*3)-1:IF DIRV=0 THEN 2070
2090    GOTO 100
```

Game end

```
4000    POSITION 4,23:? SCORE1;:POSITION 34,23:? SCORE2;
4005    POSITION 0,23:FOR T=1 TO 22:? :FOR Z=1 TO 50 STEP 4:SOU
        ND 0,Z,10,9:NEXT Z:NEXT T
4006    FOR Z=255 TO 0 STEP -1:SOUND 0,Z,10,9:NEXT Z:SOUND 0,0,
        0,0
4010    POSITION 10,9:? "Game▲over":? :? :? "Press▲<RETURN>▲for
        ▲another▲game."
4020    INPUT X$
4030    RUN
```

Draw court

```
5000    ? CHR$(125):POSITION 0,0:? WALL$;:POSITION 0,22:? WALL$
        ;
5010    POSITION 0,10:? "▲"
5020    FOR T=1 TO 21:POSITION 20,T:? ":";:NEXT T:IF  NOT PRACT
         THEN RETURN
5030    FOR T=1 TO 21:POSITION 38,T:? "|";:NEXT T:RETURN
```

Intialization routine

```
20000   SETCOLOR 4,12,2:SETCOLOR 1,12,14:SETCOLOR 2,12,2:? CHR$
        (125)
20010   SCREEN=40000
20020   DIM X$(9)
21000   PRACT=0:? :? :? :? "[P]ractice▲or▲[G]ame";:INPUT X$
21010   IF X$<>"P" AND X$<>"p" AND X$<>"G" AND X$<>"g" THEN ? :
        ? :? "SAY▲WHAT????":? :? :GOTO 21000
21020   IF X$="P" OR X$="p" THEN PRACT=1
22000   DIM WALL$(40):FOR T=2 TO 40:WALL$(T,T)=CHR$(160):NEXT T
        :WALL$(1,1)="▲"
22040   BAT1=10:BAT2=10
22050   BALL=84
22060   QZ=7.5
23000   SERVE=1:GOTO 2000
```

ChexSum Tables

10 = 461	1020 = 811	5010 = 328
20 = 1910	1030 = 543	5020 = 1569
30 = 1780	2000 = 819	5030 = 1390
100 = 1996	2010 = 1192	20000 = 1672
110 = 1376	2020 = 1053	20010 = 1426
120 = 1402	2030 = 1161	20020 = 386
140 = 1234	2035 = 1791	21000 = 2759
142 = 1385	2040 = 902	21010 = 2916
150 = 1411	2050 = 753	21020 = 1079
160 = 2415	2060 = 835	22000 = 2982
170 = 2516	2070 = 1399	22040 = 734
190 = 2112	2090 = 112	22050 = 481
200 = 1209	4000 = 1192	22060 = 429
210 = 4147	4005 = 2546	23000 = 517
240 = 1681	4006 = 1615	
250 = 1017	4010 = 4414	
900 = 1057	4020 = 178	TOTAL = 72218
1000 = 868	4030 = 59	
1010 = 871	5000 = 1327	

ROCK COLLECTOR

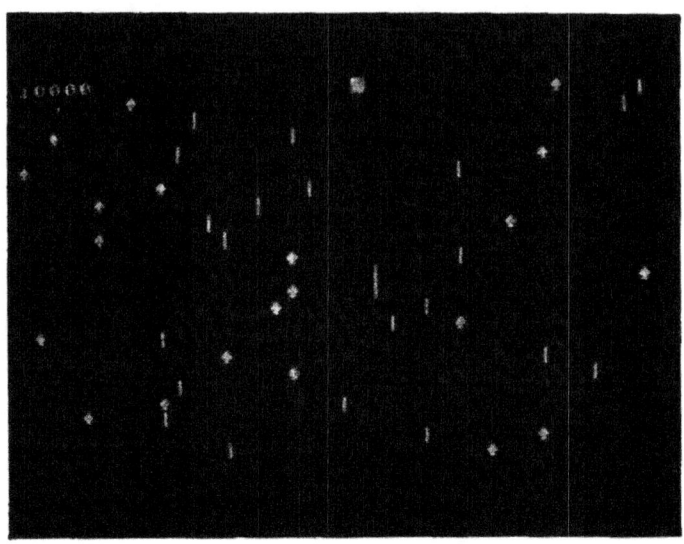

CLASSIFICATION: Evasion

Collect as many rocks as you can in the time allowed. If you hit five spikes you die. Use the I to move left and P to move right.

PROGRAMMING SUGGESTIONS

Add new objects with different score values.
Make the game work for two players at once.

Program Variables

X	Your position	B	Your position in screen RAM
SCORE	Your current score		
DEATH	Lives left	COU	Counter
BRIGHT	Time left	T,A,S,A$	Local variables

Program Structure

10 -	50	Inialization	500 - 660	Crash into object
100 -	250	Main loop	1000 - 1520	Game over

Listing

Inialization

```
10      GRAPHICS 0:POKE 752,255
20      X=20
30      DEATH=5
40      BRIGHT=15
50      COU=8
```

Main loop

```
100     POSITION INT(RND(1)*40),23
110     PRINT "♠";
120     POSITION INT(RND(1)*40),23
130     PRINT "|"
140     B=40000+X
150     IF PEEK(B)<>0 THEN GOSUB 500
160     POKE B,128
170     COU=COU-1
180     IF COU<0 THEN COU=8:BRIGHT=BRIGHT-1:SETCOLOR 4,0,BRIGHT
        :IF  NOT BRIGHT THEN GOTO 1000
190     X=X+((PEEK(754)=10) OR (STICK(0)=7))-((PEEK(754)=13) OR
        (STICK(0)=11)):- X<5 OR X>38 THEN X=20
200     POSITION 0,0.PRINT SCORE
250     GOTO 100
```

Crash into object

```
500     IF PEEK(B)=124 THEN GOTO 600
510     FOR T=30 TO 0 STEP -5
520     SOUND 0,T,10,10:SOUND 1,255-T,10,10
530     SETCOLOR 1,4,T/2
540     NEXT T
550     SOUND 0,0,0,0:SETCOLOR 1,4,10:SOUND 1,0,0,0
560     SCORE=SCORE+1000
570     POSITION 0,0:PRINT SCORE
580     RETURN
600     FOR T=0 TO 50 STEP 5
610     SOUND 0,T,10,10:SOUND 1,255-T,10,10
620     SETCOLOR 4,0,T/2
630     NEXT T:SOUND 1,0,0,0:SOUND 0,0,0,0
640     SETCOLOR 4,0,BRIGHT
650     DEATH=DEATH-1
660     IF DEATH THEN RETURN
```

> Game over

```
1000  FOR T=0 TO 250
1010  SOUND 0,T,10,7
1020  SOUND 1,T+1,10,7
1030  SOUND 2,T+2,10,7
1040  SOUND 3,T+3,10,7
1050  NEXT T
1060  FOR A=1 TO 20
1070  FOR T=0 TO 15
1080  SETCOLOR 1,8,T
1090  SETCOLOR 2,15-T,8
1100  SETCOLOR 4,T,10
1110  NEXT T
1120  NEXT A
1130  SOUND 0,0,0,0:SOUND 1,0,0,0:SOUND 2,0,0,0:SOUND 3,0,0,0
1140  DIM A$(20)
1150  GRAPHICS 18
1160  A$="GAME▴OVER":S=5:GOSUB 1500
1170  A$="YOU▴SCORED":S=5:GOSUB 1500
1180  A$=STR$(SCORE):A$(LEN(A$),LEN(A$)+7)="▴POINTS":S=4:GOSUB 1500
1190  POP :RUN
1500  FOR T=0 TO 11:POSITION S,T:PRINT #6;A$:SOUND 0,T,10,8:SOUND 1,200-T,10,10:NEXT T
1510  FOR T=0 TO 11:POSITION 0,T:PRINT #6;"▴▴▴▴▴▴▴▴▴▴▴▴▴▴":NEXT T
1520  RETURN
```

ChexSum Tables

10 = 513	530 = 520	1070 = 347
20 = 359	540 = 165	1080 = 405
30 = 333	550 = 946	1090 = 543
40 = 350	560 = 519	1100 = 416
50 = 338	570 = 323	1110 = 165
100 = 811	580 = 58	1120 = 166
110 = 214	600 = 515	1130 = 1235
120 = 811	610 = 1258	1140 = 391
130 = 194	620 = 455	1150 = 167
140 = 502	630 = 706	1160 = 1455
150 = 528	640 = 332	1170 = 1561
160 = 323	650 = 496	1180 = 2869
170 = 500	660 = 231	1190 = 127
180 = 1975	1000 = 409	1500 = 2634
190 = 3863	1010 = 453	1510 = 1739
200 = 323	1020 = 634	1520 = 58
250 = 112	1030 = 636	
500 = 633	1040 = 638	
510 = 537	1050 = 165	TOTAL = 38638
520 = 1258	1060 = 424	

SNAKES

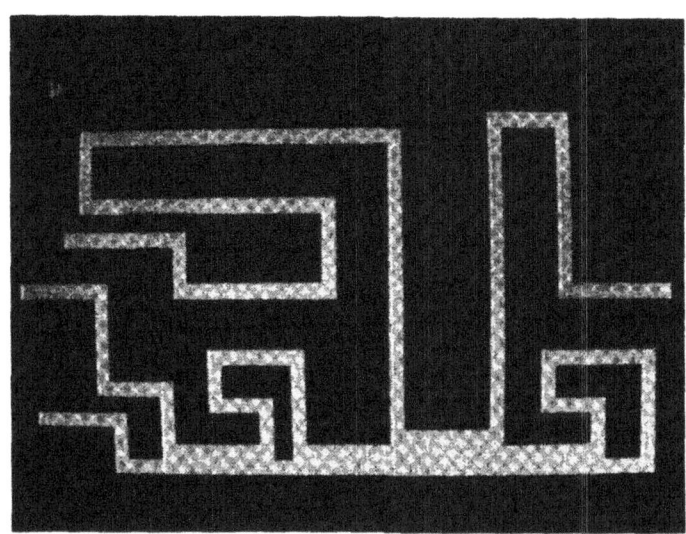

CLASSIFICATION: Strategy

This is a two player game where each player must use all his skill and intelligence to make his opponent crash into himself, the side of the screen, or the other snake. Player One uses the keyboard and Player Two uses the joystick.

PROGRAMMING SUGGESTIONS

If you wanted, you could add a third player (he would have to use joystick port 2), or you could add some kind of scoring system.

Program Variables

X1,Y1	Player One's Co-ordinates
X2,Y2	Player Two's Co-ordinates
DX1,DY1	Player One's Direction
DX2,DX2	Player Two's Direction
PI1$,PI2$	Names of players one & two

Program Structure

Line
```
  10 -   30   Initialisation
 100 -  280   Main loop
1000 - 1050   Player One's death
2000 - 2050   Player Two's death
7000 - 8000   Ask Player's names
```

Listing

Initialisation

```
10    GOSUB 7000:GRAPHICS 0:POKE 752,255
20    X1=0:Y1=12:X2=39:Y2=12
30    DX1=1:DY1=0:DX2=-1:DY2=0
```

Main loop

```
100   POKE 40000+X1+Y1*40,128
110   POKE 40000+X2+Y2*40,128
120   IF (PEEK(754)=13) THEN DX1=-1:DY1=0
130   IF (STICK(0)=11) THEN DX2=-1:DY2=0
140   IF (PEEK(754)=10) THEN DX1=1:DY1=0
150   IF (STICK(0)=7) THEN DX2=1:DY2=0
160   IF (PEEK(754)=47) THEN DX1=0:DY1=-1
170   IF (STICK(0)=14) THEN DX2=0:DY2=-1
180   IF (PEEK(754)=23) THEN DX1=0:DY1=1
190   IF (STICK(0)=13) THEN DX2=0:DY2=1
200   X1=X1+DX1:IF (X1<0 OR X1>39) OR (Y1<0 OR Y1>23) THEN GO
      TO 1000
210   X2=X2+DX2
220   Y1=Y1+DY1
230   Y2=Y2+DY2
240   IF PEEK(40000+X1+Y1*40)=128 THEN GOTO 1000
250   IF PEEK(40000+X2+Y2*40)=128 THEN GOTO 2000
260   IF (X1<0 OR X1>39) OR (Y1<0 OR Y1>23) THEN GOTO 1000
270   IF (X2<0 OR X2>39) OR (Y2<0 OR Y2>23) THEN GOTO 2000
280   GOTO 100
```

Player One's death

```
1000  GRAPHICS 18
1010  ? #6:? #6:? #6:? #6:"▲▲";PL1$;" IS DEAD."
1020  ? #6:? #6:"▲▲";PL2$;" HAS WON"
1030  POKE 754,0
1040  FOR T=0 TO 100:SOUND 1,T,0,10:IF PEEK(754)=0 THEN NEXT
      T:GOTO 1040
1050  RUN
```

> Player Two's death

```
2000   GRAPHICS 18
2010   ? #6:? #6:? #6:? #6;"▲▲";PL2$;"▲IS▲DEAD."
2020   ? #6:? #6;"▲▲";PL1$;"▲HAS▲WON"
2030   POKE 754,0
2040   FOR T=0 TO 100:SOUND 1,T,0,10:IF PEEK(754)=0 THEN NEXT
       T:GOTO 2040
2050   RUN
```

> Ask Player's names

```
7000   DIM PL1$(8),A$(40),PL2$(8)
7010   GRAPHICS 2:POSITION 0,5:? #6;"PLAYER▲1▲NAME▲?":? #6;"(M
       AX.▲8▲CHARACTERS)"
7030   INPUT A$
7040   IF LEN(A$)>8 THEN GRAPHICS 18:POSITION 0,6:? #6;"SHORTE
       N▲IT,YOU▲FOOL!":FOR T=0 TO 1000:NEXT T:GOTO 7010
7050   PL1$=A$
7060   GRAPHICS 2:POSITION 0,5:? #6;"PLAYER▲2▲NAME▲?":? #6;"(M
       AX.▲8▲CHARACTERS)"
7070   INPUT A$
7080   IF LEN(A$)>8 THEN GRAPHICS 18:POSITION 0,6:? #6;"SHORTE
       N▲IT,YOU▲FOOL!":FOR T=0 TO 1000:NEXT T:GOTO 7050
7090   PL2$=A$
8000   RETURN
```

ChexSum Tables

10 = 769	230 = 555	2040 = 1862
20 = 1454	240 = 1126	2050 = 59
30 = 1371	250 = 1146	7000 = 1113
100 = 784	260 = 1437	7010 = 3130
110 = 788	270 = 1461	7030 = 163
120 = 1336	280 = 112	7040 = 3659
130 = 1194	1000 = 167	7050 = 397
140 = 1277	1010 = 1657	7060 = 3131
150 = 1128	1020 = 1221	7070 = 163
160 = 1387	1030 = 255	7080 = 3723
170 = 1196	1040 = 1846	7090 = 398
180 = 1296	1050 = 59	8000 = 58
190 = 1140	2000 = 167	
200 = 2046	2010 = 1658	
210 = 552	2020 = 1220	TOTAL = 50465
220 = 549	2030 = 255	

DIAMOND HUNT

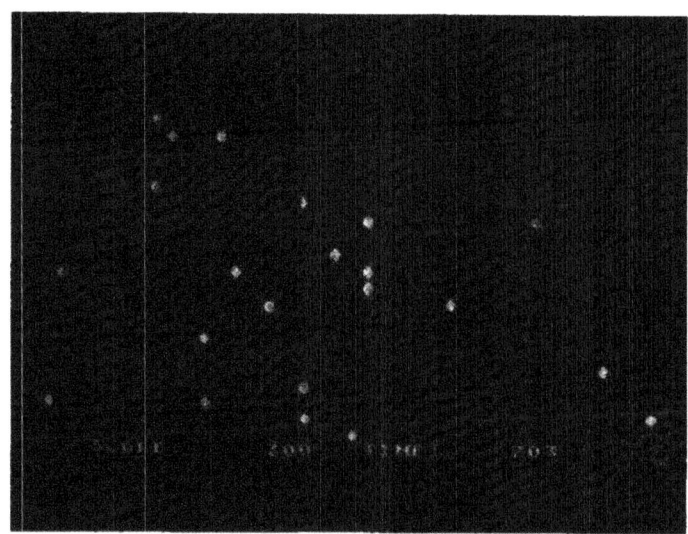

CLASSIFICATION: Reflex

In the time allowed, you must collect all the diamonds you can. If you crash into a rock, five more diamonds will be scattered across the screen, but time will be taken away.

PROGRAMMING SUGGESTIONS

Increase the speed of your man as you collect more and more diamonds.

Program Variables

X	The X coordinate
Y	The Y coordinate
SCORE	Your score
TIME	The time you have left
U	Character you have crashed into
S,S1	Music data
S2	Flag to indicate end of music
FLAG1,FLAG2	Flags for sound effects
NOISE,NOISE1	Sound effect pitches
T	Dummy variable

Program Structure

10 - 50	Initialize the game
100 - 250	Main loop
500 - 600	Hit the diamond
1000 - 1040	Hit a rock
2000 - 2050	The time is up
5000 - 5070	Music data
6000 - 6060	Draw the title screen

Listing

5   GOSUB 6000

> Initialize the game

```
10    POKE 752,255:GRAPHICS 0
20    X=0:Y=1
30    FOR T=0 TO 9:POKE 40000+INT(RND(1)*880),84:POKE 40000+I
      NT(RND(1)*880),96:NEXT T
40    SCORE=0:TIME=999
50    POSITION 0,22:PRINT "▲▲▲▲SCORE:▲▲▲▲▲▲▲▲▲▲▲▲TIME:"
```

> Main loop

```
100   POKE 40000+X+Y*40,0
110   Y=Y+((PEEK(754)=23) OR (STICK(0)=13))-((PEEK(754)=47) O
      R (STICK(0)=14))
120   IF Y<0 THEN Y=21
130   IF Y>21 THEN Y=0
140   X=X+1:IF X>39 THEN X=0
150   U=PEEK(40000+X+Y*40)
160   POKE 40000+X+Y*40,127
170   IF U=96 THEN GOSUB 500
180   IF U=84 THEN GOSUB 1000
190   TIME=TIME-1:POSITION 30,22:? TIME;"▲";:IF TIME<1 THEN G
      OTO 2000
200   READ S,S1,S2:SOUND 0,S,10,10:SOUND 1,S1,10,10:IF S2 THE
      N RESTORE
210   IF FLAG1 THEN NOISE=NOISE-1:SOUND 2,NOISE,8,13:SETCOLOR
      1,8,INT(RND(1)*15):IF NOISE<1 THEN FLAG1=0:SOUND 2,0,0
      ,0:SETCOLOR 1,13,10
220   IF FLAG2 THEN NOISE1=NOISE1-10:SOUND 3,NOISE1,10,10:IF
      NOISE1<1 THEN NOISE1=30:FLAG2=FLAG2-1:IF FLAG2=0 THEN S
      OUND 3,0,0,0
230   IF FLAG2 THEN SETCOLOR 2,INT(RND(1)*15),3
240   IF NOT FLAG2 THEN SETCOLOR 2,11,5
250   GOTO 100
```

> Hit the diamond

```
500   SCORE=SCORE+50
510   POSITION 15,22:? SCORE;
520   NOISE1=30:FLAG2=4
600   RETURN
```

```
1000    FOR T=0 TO 4
1010    POKE 40000+INT(RND(1)*880),96
1020    NEXT T
1030    TIME=TIME-20
1035    NOISE=10:FLAG1=1
1040    RETURN
```

The time is up

```
2000    GRAPHICS 18:SOUND 0,0,0,0:SOUND 1,0,0,0:SOUND 2,0,0,0:S
        OUND 3,0,0,0
2010    ? #6:? #6:? #6:? #6;"▲▲▲▲▲▲TIME▲UP!"
2020    ? #6:? #6;"YOUR▲SCORE▲WAS▲";SCORE
2030    POKE 754,0
2040    SOUND 0,INT(RND(1)*30),7,10:SOUND 1,INT(RND(1)*255),4,1
        0:IF PEEK(754)=0 THEN GOTO 2040
2050    RUN
```

Music data

```
5000    DATA 162,81,0,162,81,0,162,81,0,162,81,0,108,81,0,108,8
        1,0,96,81,0,96,81,0,96,81,0,96,81,0,108,81,0,108,81,0
5010    DATA 162,81,0,162,81,0,162,81,0,162,81,0,108,81,0,108,8
        1,0,96,72,0,96,72,0,96,72,0,96,72,0,108,72,0,108,64,0
5020    DATA 162,64,0,162,64,0,162,53,0,162,53,0,108,53,0,108,5
        3,0,96,53,0,96,53,0,96,53,0,96,53,0,108,53,0,108,53,0
5030    DATA 162,53,0,162,53,0,162,53,0,162,53,0,108,53,0,108,5
        3,0,96,64,0,96,64,0,96,72,0,96,72,0,108,81,0,108,81,0
5040    DATA 162,64,0,162,64,0,162,64,0,162,64,0,108,64,0,108,6
        4,0,96,64,0,96,64,0,96,64,0,96,64,0,108,64,0,108,64,0
5050    DATA 162,64,0,162,64,0,162,64,0,162,64,0,108,64,0,108,6
        4,0,96,72,0,96,72,0,96,72,0,96,72,0,108,72,0,108,72,0
5060    DATA 162,81,0,162,81,0,162,81,0,162,81,0,108,81,0,108,8
        1,0,96,81,0,96,81,0,96,81,0,96,81,0,108,81,0,108,81,0
5070    DATA 162,81,0,162,81,0,162,81,0,162,81,0,108,81,0,108,8
        1,0,96,81,0,96,81,0,96,0,0,96,0,0,108,0,0,108,0,1
```

Draw the title screen

```
6000    GRAPHICS 18
6005    POKE 754,0
6010    FOR T=0 TO 11:POSITION T,5:? #6;"▲DIAMOND▲":NEXT T
6015    FOR T=0 TO 30 STEP 10:SOUND 1,T,0,15:NEXT T:SOUND 1,0,0
        ,0
6020    FOR T=10 TO 1 STEP -1:POSITION T,5:? #6;"▲DIAMOND▲":NEX
        T T
6030    FOR T=0 TO 15:POSITION T,7:? #6;"▲HUNT":NEXT T
6035    FOR T=0 TO 30 STEP 10:SOUND 1,T,0,15:NEXT T:SOUND 1,0,0
        ,0
```

```
6040    FOR T=14 TO 1 STEP -1:POSITION T,7:? #6;" HUNT ":NEXT T

6050    IF PEEK(754)<>0 THEN RETURN
6060    GOTO 6010
```

ChexSum Tables

```
  5 = 209          240 = 611         5020 = 5192
 10 = 513          250 = 112         5030 = 5196
 20 = 617          500 = 578         5040 = 5212
 30 = 2953         510 = 534         5050 = 5206
 40 = 785          520 = 754         5060 = 5200
 50 = 1635         600 = 58          5070 = 4973
100 = 678         1000 = 326         6000 = 167
110 = 2731        1010 = 1106        6005 = 255
120 = 597         1020 = 161         6010 = 1738
130 = 598         1030 = 533         6015 = 1559
140 = 1154        1035 = 715         6020 = 1988
150 = 1019        1040 = 58          6030 = 1511
160 = 783         2000 = 1477        6035 = 1559
170 = 572         2010 = 1590        6040 = 1796
180 = 565         2020 = 1640        6050 = 505
190 = 1724        2030 = 255         6060 = 223
200 = 1959        2040 = 2910
210 = 3915        2050 = 59
220 = 3414        5000 = 5200
230 = 1057        5010 = 5201        TOTAL = 93636
```

SPACMAN

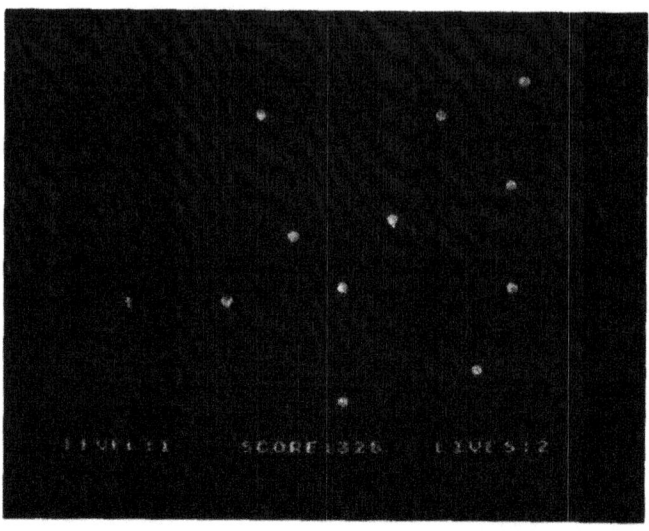

CLASSIFICATION: Invader/Evasion

Collect all of the objects on the screen and avoid the love heart. Use the I,P,Q and Z keys to move left,right,up and down.

PROGRAMMING SUGGESTIONS

Increase the speed of the game by resorting to machine code.

Program Variables

SCORE	Your score.
LEVEL	The level you are at in the game.
LIVES	The number of lives left
X,Y	Your player's coordinates on the screen
A,B	The love hearts X and Y coordinates
OBJ	Number of objects collected
T	Dummy variables
VA	Character under love heart
UY	Character under you

Program Structure

Lines

5 -	80	Initailization
100 -	250	Main loop
500 -	580	Get object
1000 -	1060	Death
5000 -	5060	Title screen

Listing

> Initailization

```
5       GOSUB 5000
10      SCORE=0:LEVEL=1:LIVES=3
```

> Initialize display

```
20      GRAPHICS 0:POKE 752,255
30      X=39:Y=21
40      A=1:B=1:OBJ=-1
50      POSITION 0,22:PRINT "▲▲▲▲LEVEL:";LEVEL;"▲▲▲▲SCORE:";
        SCORE;"▲▲▲LIVES:";LIVES
60      FOR T=0 TO (LEVEL*2+10):POKE 40000+INT(RND(1)*819),84:N
        EXT T
70      UA=PEEK(40000+A+B*40):UY=PEEK(40000+X+Y*40)
80      IF UY=84 THEN GOSUB 500
```

> Main loop

```
100     POKE 40000+A+B*40,UA
110     A=A+(X>A)-(X<A):B=B+(Y>B)-(Y<B)
120     UA=PEEK(40000+A+B*40):IF UA=92 THEN GOTO 1000
130     POKE 40000+A+B*40,64
140     POKE 40000+X+Y*40,UY
150     X=X+((PEEK(754)=10) OR (STICK(0)=7))-((PEEK(754)=13) OR
         (STICK(0)=11))
160     IF X>39 THEN X=0
170     IF X<0 THEN X=39
180     Y=Y+((PEEK(754)=23) OR (STICK(0)=13))-((PEEK(754)=47) O
        R (STICK(0)=14))
190     IF Y>21 THEN Y=0
200     IF Y<0 THEN Y=21
210     UY=PEEK(40000+X+Y*40)
220     POKE 40000+X+Y*40,92
230     IF ((A=X) AND (B=Y)) AND (UA<>84) THEN GOTO 1000
240     IF UY=84 THEN GOSUB 500
250     GOTO 100
```

```
500   UY=0:OBJ=OBJ+1:SCORE=SCORE+25:POSITION 21,22:? SCORE;
505   FOR T=0 TO 30 STEP 2:SOUND 1,T,0,9:NEXT T:SOUND 1,0,0,0

510   IF OBJ<>(LEVEL*2+10) THEN RETURN
520   GRAPHICS 18
530   ? #6:? #6:? #6:? #6:? #6;"▲▲▲▲▲▲WELL▲DONE!"
540   FOR T=0 TO 300:NEXT T
550   GRAPHICS 18
560   LEVEL=LEVEL+1
570   ? #6:? #6:? #6:? #6:? #6;"▲▲▲▲▲▲LEVEL▲";LEVEL
580   FOR T=0 TO 255:SOUND 1,T,10,10:NEXT T:POP :SOUND 1,0,0,
      0:GOTO 20
```

Death

```
1000  LIVES=LIVES-1
1005  FOR N=0 TO 5:FOR T=255 TO 200 STEP -5:SOUND 1,T,10,10:S
      OUND 0,T-200,0,9:NEXT T:NEXT N:SOUND 1,0,0,0:SOUND 0,0,
      0,0
1010  IF LIVES THEN GOTO 20
1020  GRAPHICS 18
1030  ? #6:? #6:? #6:? #6;"▲▲▲▲▲YOU▲ARE▲DEAD."
1031  FOR T=0 TO 10:SOUND 1,0,0,0:READ A,B:SOUND 1,A,10,10:FO
      R N=1 TO B:NEXT N:NEXT T:SOUND 1,0,0,0
1032  DATA 108,80,108,80,108,40,108,80,91,80,96,40,96,80,108,
      40,108,80,114,40,108,160
1040  POKE 754,0
1050  IF PEEK(754)=0 THEN GOTO 1050
1060  RUN
```

Title screen

```
5000  GRAPHICS 0:SETCOLOR 2,12,4
5010  POSITION 0,5
5015  POKE 754,0
5020  ? "▲▲▲▲";
```

Graphics for title

```
5030  ? "▲▄▀▀▀▄▄▀▀▀▄▄▀▀▀▄▄▀▀▀▄▄▀▀▀▄▄▀▀▀▄▄▀▀▀▄▄▲▲▲▲▲▲▲▲▲▲
      ▄▀▄▄▀▀▄▄▀▄▀▄▄▄▄▄▄▀▀▀▄▄▄▄▄▄▄▄▄▄▄▄▄▄▄▄▄▄▄▄▄▀▄▄
      ▄▄▄▄▄▄▀▀▀▄▀▀▀▄▄▄▄▄▄▄▄▄▄▄▄▄▄"
```

142

```
5040    ? :? :SETCOLOR 1,0,INT(RND(1)*15)
5045    SOUND 0,INT(RND(1)*255),0,10
5046    FOR T=0 TO 255 STEP 16
5047    SOUND 1,T,10,10
5048    NEXT T
5050    IF PEEK(754)>0 THEN SOUND 0,0,0,0:SOUND 1,0,0,0:RETURN
5060    GOTO 5020
```

ChexSum Tables

5 = 193	210 = 1030	1031 = 3165
10 = 986	220 = 894	1032 = 3804
20 = 513	230 = 1609	1040 = 255
30 = 776	240 = 559	1050 = 665
40 = 1119	250 = 112	1060 = 59
50 = 2565	500 = 2019	5000 = 480
60 = 2015	505 = 1551	5010 = 182
70 = 2118	510 = 750	5015 = 255
80 = 559	520 = 167	5020 = 230
100 = 811	530 = 1958	5030 = 4248
110 = 2501	540 = 524	5040 = 947
120 = 1681	550 = 167	5045 = 885
130 = 852	560 = 495	5046 = 542
140 = 808	570 = 1843	5047 = 529
150 = 2649	580 = 1910	5048 = 167
160 = 626	1000 = 498	5050 = 1151
170 = 625	1005 = 3601	5060 = 223
180 = 2737	1010 = 323	
190 = 604	1020 = 167	TOTAL = 65153
200 = 603	1030 = 1848	

MAZING

CLASSIFICATION: Evasion

Move your man around the screen with joystick 1. You must eat all of the asterisks. When you have eaten all of the asterisks you will move onto the next level. A nasty little beastie will try to eat you while you are moving round the board. Beware!!!!

PROGRAMMING SUGGESTIONS

Increase the number of nasties moving round the screen and add music to the background to make the game more interesting.

Program Variables

BDIR	Beast direction
BPOS	Beast position
BX	Beast X position
BY	Beast Y position
FLAGS	Sound flag
HITFLAG	Indicates a hit
LEVEL	Current level
M$	Holds the maze
MAN	CHR$ code for man
NUMMEN	Number of men
OLDB	Beasts old position
OLDCHR	Character under beast
OLDPLACE	Mans old screen position
PLACE	Mans position on screen
POSH	Mans X position
POSV	Mans Y position
RAND	Where to PEEK for a random number
SCREEN	Start of video RAM

Program Structure

10	Cursor off and set margins
20	Jump to initialization
100 - 212	Move man
1000 - 1500	Move beastie
2000 - 2030	Put man on board
3000	Hit something
3010 - 3080	Update condition
3100 - 3230	Hit the beastie
3500 - 3580	All the men are gone
4000 - 4040	End of the game
9000 - 9330	Put maze level into M$
9500 - 9520	Convert maze to screen format
9530 - 9590	Put the asterisks into maze
9600 - 9690	Draw the maze
10001 - 10024	Data for maze one
10051 - 10074	Data for maze two
10100 - 10124	Data for maze three
10151 - 10174	Data for maze four
20000 - 20110	Initialize the subroutines

Listing

```
1     REM ......... NOTE :LAST LINE IN EACH  DATA BLOCK IS 1
      CHARACTER SHORTER THAN  THE REST ...................
      ........
10    POKE 752,1:POKE 82,0:POKE 83,39
20    GOTO 20000
100   TIME=TIME+1:PLACE=SCREEN+POSH+POSV*40:OLDPLACE=PLACE:PO
      KE 77,0
110   Z=STICK(0):IF FLAGS THEN SOUND 0,FLAGS,10,12:FLAGS=FLAG
      S-5:IF FLAGS<20 THEN FLAGS=0
120   IF FLAGS=0 THEN SOUND 0,255,10,12
130   ON Z GOTO 1000,1000,1000,1000,190,180,140,1000,200,210,
      150,1000,160,170,1000
140   IF PEEK(PLACE+1)<>128 THEN POSH=POSH+1
141   GOTO 1000
150   IF PEEK(PLACE-1)<>128 THEN POSH=POSH-1
151   GOTO 1000
160   IF PEEK(PLACE+40)<>128 THEN POSV=POSV+1
161   GOTO 1000
170   IF PEEK(PLACE-40)<>128 THEN POSV=POSV-1
171   GOTO 1000
180   IF PEEK(PLACE-39)<>128 THEN POSV=POSV-1:POSH=POSH+1:GOT
      O 1000
181   IF PEEK(PLACE-40)<>128 THEN POSV=POSV-1:GOTO 1000
182   IF PEEK(PLACE+1)<>128 THEN POSH=POSH+1
183   GOTO 1000
190   IF PEEK(PLACE+41)<>128 THEN POSV=POSV+1:POSH=POSH+1:GOT
      O 1000
191   IF PEEK(PLACE+40)<>128 THEN POSV=POSV+1:GOTO 1000
192   IF PEEK(PLACE+1)<>128 THEN POSH=POSH+1
193   GOTO 1000
200   IF PEEK(PLACE+39)<>128 THEN POSV=POSV+1:POSH=POSH-1:GOT
      O 1000
201   IF PEEK(PLACE-1)<>128 THEN POSH=POSH-1:GOTO 1000
202   IF PEEK(PLACE+40)<>128 THEN POSV=POSV+1:GOTO 1000
203   GOTO 1000
210   IF PEEK(PLACE-41)<>128 THEN POSH=POSH-1:POSV=POSV-1:GOT
      O 1000
211   IF PEEK(PLACE-1)<>128 THEN POSH=POSH-1:GOTO 1000
212   IF PEEK(PLACE-40)<>128 THEN POSV=POSV-1:GOTO 1000
```

```
                                  | Move beastie |
```

```
1000  T=BPOS-SCREEN
1210  BY=INT(T/40):BX=T-40*BY
1220  OLDB=BPOS
1230  IF ABS(BDIR)=1 THEN GOTO 1270
1240  T=SGN(POSH-BX):IF T AND PEEK(BPOS+T)<>128 AND PEEK(RAND
      )>220 THEN 1380
1250  IF T AND PEEK(BPOS+T)<>128 THEN BDIR=T:GOTO 1450
```

```
1260    GOTO 1290
1270    T=40*SGN(POSV-BY):IF T AND PEEK(BPOS+T)<>128 AND PEEK(R
        AND)>220 THEN 1380
1280    IF T AND PEEK(BPOS+T)<>128 THEN BDIR=T:GOTO 1450
1290    IF PEEK(BPOS+BDIR)<>128 THEN GOTO 1450
1300    T=PEEK(RAND)>127
1310    IF T THEN GOTO 1340
1320    T=SGN(POSH-BX)
1330    IF T AND PEEK(BPOS+T)<>128 THEN BDIR=T:GOTO 1450
1340    T=40*SGN(POSV-BY)
1350    IF T AND PEEK(BPOS+T)<>128 THEN BDIR=T:GOTO 1450
1360    T=SGN(HPOS-BX)
1370    IF T AND PEEK(BPOS+T)<>128 THEN BDIR=T:GOTO 1450
1380    T=INT(RND(0)*4)
1390    ON T GOTO 1410,1420,1430
1400    IF PEEK(BPOS-40)<>128 THEN BDIR=-40:GOTO 1450
1410    IF PEEK(BPOS+40)<>128 THEN BDIR=40:GOTO 1450
1420    IF PEEK(BPOS-1)<>128 THEN BDIR=-1:GOTO 1450
1430    IF PEEK(BPOS+1)<>128 THEN BDIR=1:GOTO 1450
1440    GOTO 1400
1450    BPOS=BPOS+BDIR
1460    POKE OLDB,OLDCHR
1470    OLDCHR=PEEK(BPOS)
1480    POKE BPOS,THEM
1490    HITFLAG=(OLDCHR=MAN)
1500    IF HITFLAG THEN 3100
```

> Put man on board

```
2000    POKE OLDPLACE,0:PLACE=SCREEN+POSH+POSV*40
2010    T=PEEK(PLACE):IF T THEN 3000
2020    POKE PLACE,MAN
2030    GOTO 100
3000    IF T<>10 THEN 3100
3010    TOTAL=TOTAL-1:T=PLACE-SCREEN+1:M$(T,T)=" ▲"
3020    FLAGS=60:IF TOTAL THEN 100
3030    FOR T=1 TO 30:? :NEXT T
3040    IF LEVEL=3 THEN 4000
3050    GRAPHICS 2+16
3060    LEVEL=LEVEL+1:POSITION 3,5:? #6;"LEVEL ▲";LEVEL+1:POSITI
        ON 3,8:? #6;NUMMEN;" ▲REMAINING"
3070    FOR T=100 TO 0 STEP -1:SOUND 0,T,12,15:NEXT T:SOUND 0,2
        55,10,12
3080    GOTO 20070
```

```
          ┌─────────────────────────┐
          │    Hit the beastie      │
          └─────────────────────────┘

3100    X=POSH+POSV*40+SCREEN
3110    FOR T=255 TO 0 STEP -1
3120    POKE X,T:SOUND 0,T,10,12
3130    NEXT T
3140    NUMMEN=NUMMEN-1
3150    IF  NOT NUMMEN THEN 3500
3160    GRAPHICS 2+16:? #6;NUMMEN;"▴▴REMAINING"
3170    POSH=25:POSV=9
3180    T1=0:T2=0:FOR T=0 TO 255:SOUND 0,T,10,12:SOUND 1,T1,10,
        12:SOUND 2,T2,10,12
3190    T1=T1+2:IF T1>255 THEN T1=0
3200    T2=T2+3:IF T2>255 THEN T2=0
3210    OLDS=T:NEXT T
3220    GOSUB 9600
3230    GOTO 100

          ┌─────────────────────────┐
          │   All the men are gone  │
          └─────────────────────────┘

3500    GRAPHICS 2+16:POSITION 2,5:? #6;"ALL▴MEN▴DEAD!!":FOR T=
        1 TO 255 STEP 4
3510    SOUND 1,0,0,0:SOUND 2,0,0,0:FOR T1=1 TO 253 STEP T
3520    SOUND 0,T1,10,12
3530    NEXT T1
3540    NEXT T
3550    SOUND 0,0,0,0
3580    GOTO 4020

          ┌─────────────────────────┐
          │     End of the game     │
          └─────────────────────────┘

4000    ? "ALL▴LEVELS▴COMPLETED!"
4010    ? :? "SCORE▴:";TIME
4020    ? :? :? "PRESS▴<RETURN>▴FOR▴ANOTHER▴GAME"
4030    INPUT X$
4040    RUN

          ┌─────────────────────────┐
          │  Put maze level into M$ │
          └─────────────────────────┘

9000    RESTORE 10000+LEVEL*50+1
9010    POSH=25:POSV=9
9100    FOR T=0 TO 23
9200    READ T$
```

```
9300    M$(T*40+1,T*40+40)=T$
9310    NEXT T
9320    GOSUB 9500:GOSUB 9600
9330    RETURN
```

> Convert maze to screen format

```
9500    FOR T=1 TO LEN(M$)
9510    IF M$(T,T)="*" THEN M$(T,T)=CHR$(160)
9520    NEXT T
```

> Put the asterisks into maze

```
9530    TOTAL=30
9540    FOR T=1 TO TOTAL
9560    Z=INT(RND(0)*959+1):IF M$(Z,Z)<>" " THEN 9560
9570    M$(Z,Z)="*"
9580    NEXT T
9590    RETURN
```

> Draw the maze

```
9600    FOR T=1 TO 20:? :NEXT T
9610    ? M$;
9620    POKE SCREEN+959,128
9640    BPOS=SCREEN+882:OLDCHR=PEEK(BPOS)
9670    BDIR=1
9690    RETURN
```

> Data for maze one

```
10001 DATA ****************************************
10002 DATA *    *    *                            *
10003 DATA * * * * * ***** ********* ****** * * **
10004 DATA * * * * *     *     *               *  *
10005 DATA * *    *   * *   * * ***** ***** ** * **
10006 DATA * *** *** *******  * *           * *   *
10007 DATA * *       *        * * *** *** * * * **
10008 DATA *** ***** * ***** * * *       * * * * *
10009 DATA *         *       * * * *** * * **** *
10010 DATA * *** *** *** *** *   *   * *   * *   *
10011 DATA * *      *      *   * * *** * * * * **
10012 DATA * * * * * *** * *** * *      *** *    *
10013 DATA * * * * *     *       * ******* * ** ***
10014 DATA * *       * *** * *** *         * *   * *
```

```
10015 DATA *  ***  ***                  *****  *****     *    **
10016 DATA *         *******  ****  *      *  *      *  ****  ***
10017 DATA ** *** * *       *        *         *        * *       *
10018 DATA *  *    *    * * *      ***************   *  *  ***
10019 DATA * ** * * * * *  *****          *       *      *      *
10020 DATA * *   *    *            * * * * *  *****  * *
10021 DATA * * *** ******* **     *      *      *            * *
10022 DATA * ***     *    *       ******************  ***  *
10023 DATA *         **   *    *                                *
10024 DATA *****************************************
```

Data for maze two

```
10051 DATA ******************************************
10052 DATA *              *              *     * *           *
10053 DATA * * * * ***** * * * * * * * * ****** *
10054 DATA * * * * *       * * * * * * * *           *
10055 DATA * * * * * ***** * * * * * * ** *******
10056 DATA * * * * * *       * * * * *    *       *
10057 DATA * * * * * * *** * * * ***** * ****** *
10058 DATA * * * * * *       *        *       *           *
10059 DATA * * * *    * *** * * * *** * ********  *
10060 DATA * * * * *       * * * * *         *
10061 DATA * * *    *    *** * * * * * **********
10062 DATA * * * * * *    * *** *    * *    *       *
10063 DATA * * *    *    * * *    * *****  ***  * ** *
10064 DATA * * * * * * * **** **  *       * * *   *
10065 DATA * * * * * *    *        * *****  * * * **
10066 DATA * * * * ******* * ***** * *    *    *    *
10067 DATA *           *          *              *    * * **
10068 DATA ****** **** *** *** *************** * *
10069 DATA *              *        *      *    * ** ** *
10070 DATA * ************* * *** * **    * * *         *
10071 DATA *              *        *      * * * * *****
10072 DATA ********* **********  * ******* * *    * *
10073 DATA *                    *              *    *** *
10074 DATA ******************************************
```

Data for maze three

```
10101 DATA ********************************************
10102 DATA *             *        *       *          *    *    *
10103 DATA * *  ** * * * *** * *** * * **     *       * *
10104 DATA * **    * * ***** * *    *  * ***********  *
10105 DATA *         *           *         **    * * *             *
10106 DATA ***** **** **** **** **** *    ** *******
10107 DATA *                                  ******       *
10108 DATA * *** *** *** *** *** ***     *******  *
10109 DATA *                                *********         *
10110 DATA *** * * * * * * * * *** *         *******
10111 DATA *                           * ****  *****       *
10112 DATA * * * * * * * * * * * *              *** *
```

```
10113 DATA *                       ******** *     *
10114 DATA * * * * * * * * * * *       *     * *******
10115 DATA *                       * ** * *           *
10116 DATA * * * * * * * * * * * * * * * *** *** *
10117 DATA *                         ** * *    *     *
10118 DATA *** ** ** ** ** ** ** ***  * * * * *** *
10119 DATA *                         * ** * * *       *
10120 DATA * ** ** ** ** ** ** ** ** * * * * *****
10121 DATA *                         *** * * * *      *
10122 DATA * *** *** *** *** *** **  * * * ***** *
10123 DATA *                           *       *     *
10124 DATA ****************************************
```

Data for maze four

```
10151 DATA ****************************************
10152 DATA *     *     *     *         *     *     * *
10153 DATA * * * * * * * * * * * * * * * * * *     **
10154 DATA * * * * * * * * * * * * * *   *   *** *
10155 DATA *   *   *   *       *   * ********** ** *
10156 DATA ** **** ** *** *********** *       *    *
10157 DATA *   *   *   *   *   * * * *****    * * **
10158 DATA * * * **** *** ***     * ** ***** * *
10159 DATA * * *       *       * * **** * *   *** **
10160 DATA * * * * * ** **********    *   *   *
10161 DATA * * * * * *     * * ***********    * *
10162 DATA * * * * * ** *** * * *   *   *******
10163 DATA * * *   * * *   * *   * * ******    * *
10164 DATA *   * * * * * **** * *** * * *   * * * *
10165 DATA * * * * * * * *       * * *   *         *
10166 DATA *   * * * * *     * * * * * * * * * * *
10167 DATA *** * * * * * ** ** ** * * *     * *   *
10168 DATA *       * *   * *     * * * * * *   * ***
10169 DATA *** * * * * ** * * * * * * * * * * *    *
10170 DATA *         *   * * *     * * * *     * * *
10171 DATA *** ** * *** * * * * * * * * * *     * * *
10172 DATA * * *   *   * * * * * * * * * * * * *    *
10173 DATA *   * ** *   *   *   *   *         *   * *
10174 DATA ****************************************
```

Initialize the subroutines

```
20000 DIM M$(960),T$(40),X$(9)
20020 LEVEL=0:TIME=0:SCREEN=40000:OLDS=0:RAND=53770
20030 GRAPHICS 2+16
20040 POSITION 5,10
20050 ? #6;"JUST A TICK."
20060 NUMMEN=3
20070 GOSUB 9000
20080 MAN=123
20090 THEM=88
20110 GOTO 100
```

ChexSum Tables

10 = 1118	1460 = 369	9530 = 378
20 = 114	1470 = 588	9540 = 445
100 = 2246	1480 = 367	9560 = 2092
110 = 2530	1490 = 700	9570 = 778
120 = 770	1500 = 337	9580 = 166
130 = 2416	2000 = 1184	9590 = 58
140 = 1164	2010 = 905	9600 = 704
141 = 127	2020 = 362	9610 = 238
150 = 1166	2030 = 112	9620 = 543
151 = 127	3000 = 443	9640 = 1269
160 = 1229	3010 = 2014	9670 = 348
161 = 127	3020 = 730	9690 = 58
170 = 1231	3030 = 720	10001 = 1836
171 = 127	3040 = 470	10002 = 1476
180 = 1980	3050 = 282	10003 = 1736
181 = 1406	3060 = 3347	10004 = 1526
182 = 1164	3070 = 1836	10005 = 1656
183 = 127	3080 = 226	10006 = 1626
190 = 1986	3100 = 948	10007 = 1596
191 = 1404	3110 = 574	10008 = 1656
192 = 1164	3120 = 864	10009 = 1586
193 = 127	3130 = 166	10010 = 1636
200 = 1979	3140 = 552	10011 = 1606
201 = 1341	3150 = 385	10012 = 1616
202 = 1404	3160 = 1457	10013 = 1646
203 = 127	3170 = 748	10014 = 1586
210 = 1989	3180 = 2952	10015 = 1636
211 = 1341	3190 = 1310	10016 = 1666
212 = 1406	3200 = 1315	10017 = 1576
1000 = 576	3210 = 594	10018 = 1676
1210 = 1561	3220 = 263	10019 = 1616
1220 = 412	3230 = 112	10020 = 1606
1230 = 745	3500 = 2378	10021 = 1626
1240 = 2417	3510 = 1318	10022 = 1706
1250 = 1528	3520 = 489	10023 = 1496
1260 = 273	3530 = 190	10024 = 1794
1270 = 2603	3540 = 166	10051 = 1836
1280 = 1528	3550 = 182	10052 = 1496
1290 = 926	3580 = 207	10053 = 1686
1300 = 729	4000 = 1540	10054 = 1586
1310 = 380	4010 = 791	10055 = 1696
1320 = 759	4020 = 2451	10056 = 1566
1330 = 1528	4030 = 186	10057 = 1696
1340 = 937	4040 = 59	10058 = 1536
1350 = 1528	9000 = 641	10059 = 1686
1360 = 770	9010 = 748	10060 = 1576
1370 = 1528	9100 = 362	10061 = 1676
1380 = 744	9200 = 219	10062 = 1596
1390 = 639	9300 = 1520	10063 = 1646
1400 = 1442	9310 = 166	10064 = 1626
1410 = 1385	9320 = 546	10065 = 1616
1420 = 1316	9330 = 58	10066 = 1666
1430 = 1259	9500 = 637	10067 = 1516
1440 = 131	9510 = 1810	10068 = 1766
1450 = 594	9520 = 166	10069 = 1536

```
10070 = 1686        10119 = 1516        10168 = 1596
10071 = 1556        10120 = 1696        10169 = 1646
10072 = 1726        10121 = 1526        10170 = 1576
10073 = 1506        10122 = 1706        10171 = 1656
10074 = 1794        10123 = 1476        10172 = 1616
10101 = 1836        10124 = 1794        10173 = 1556
10102 = 1506        10151 = 1836        10174 = 1794
10103 = 1646        10152 = 1536        20000 = 1280
10104 = 1696        10153 = 1636        20020 = 1895
10105 = 1526        10154 = 1626        20030 = 282
10106 = 1746        10155 = 1616        20040 = 262
10107 = 1516        10156 = 1676        20050 = 1022
10108 = 1706        10157 = 1606        20060 = 359
10109 = 1536        10158 = 1666        20070 = 257
10110 = 1656        10159 = 1606        20080 = 390
10111 = 1556        10160 = 1636        20090 = 487
10112 = 1596        10161 = 1656        20110 = 112
10113 = 1546        10162 = 1656
10114 = 1646        10163 = 1616
10115 = 1506        10164 = 1646        TOTAL = 275698
10116 = 1656        10165 = 1576
10117 = 1506        10166 = 1616
10118 = 1696        10167 = 1646
```

WORMA

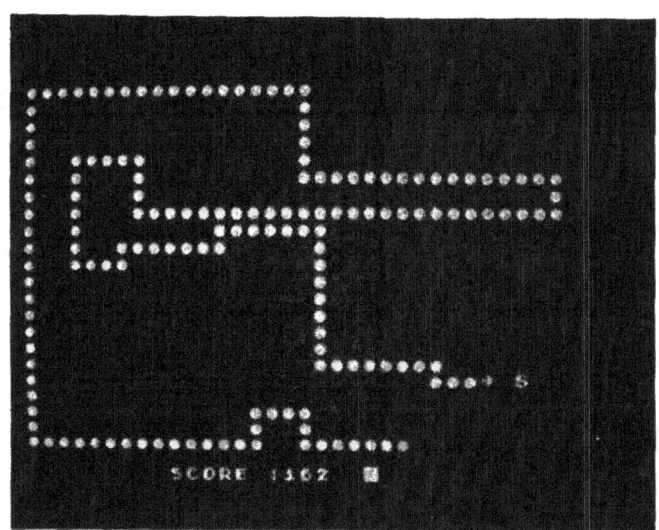

CLASSIFICATION: Skill

You must move your worm around the screen for as long as possible. When a number appears, run over it and the tail of your worm will grow longer. The joystick controls the direction of the worms head and pressing the fire button sends the worm in that direction. If your head touches your body then game is over. The objective of this game is to live as long as possible and make the worm grow to the maximium length.

PROGRAMMING SUGGESTIONS

Increase the speed that the worm moves around the board and put fatal obstacles in its path.

Program Variables

AMX( )	Amounts to move X
AMY( )	Amounts to move Y
BODY	Screen code for body
CHANGE	Flag position change
DROP	Number of times to grow
FRONT	Screen codes for arrows
HEAD	Position of head in array
POS	Screen position of head
POST	Used to put number on screen
SCREEN	Start of video ram
TAIL	Position of tail in array
TYPE	Direction indicater
X( )	X coordinates of worm
Y( )	Y coordinates of worm

Program Structure

10 -	Jump initialize
100 - 200	Main loop
5000 - 5060	Joystick routine
5200 - 5320	Move routine
6000 - 6050	Random number to screen
10000 - 10070	End of game
20000 - 20170	Initialize

Listing

```
10   POKE 752,2:? :GOTO 20000
100  POKE 77,0:ZQ=X(HEAD)+40*Y(HEAD)+SCREEN:GOSUB 5000
110  POS=X(HEAD)+40*Y(HEAD)+SCREEN
120  Q=PEEK(POS):IF Q=BODY THEN 10000
130  IF Q>16 AND Q<26 THEN Q=Q-16:DROP=DROP+Q:SCORE=SCORE+Q:
     TEST=0
140  IF CHANGE AND  NOT DROP THEN TAIL=TAIL-1:IF TAIL<0 THEN
      TAIL=970
150  IF CHANGE AND DROP THEN DROP=DROP-1
160  POKE X(TAIL)+40*Y(TAIL)+SCREEN,0
170  Z=HEAD+1: IF Z>970 THEN Z=0
180  IF HEAD<>TAIL THEN POKE X(Z)+40*Y(Z)+SCREEN,BODY
181  IF HEAD=TAIL THEN POKE ZQ,0
190  POKE X(HEAD)+40*Y(HEAD)+SCREEN,FRONT(TYPE)
200  IF  NOT TEST THEN GOSUB 6000
210  POSITION 10,23:? "SCORE▲:";SCORE;"▲▲";
220  GOTO 100
```

```
                         ┌─────────────────────────┐
                         │   Joystick routine      │
                         └─────────────────────────┘
```

```
5000  S=STICK(0)
5010  IF S=15 THEN 5200
5020  ON S GOTO 5200,5200,5200,5200,5200,5200,5040,5200,5200,
      5200,5060,5200,5050,5030,5200
5030  TYPE=0:GOTO 5200
5040  TYPE=3:GOTO 5200
5050  TYPE=1:GOTO 5200
5060  TYPE=2:GOTO 5200
```

```
                         ┌─────────────────────────┐
                         │    Move routine         │
                         └─────────────────────────┘
```

```
5200  CHANGE=0
5210  IF STRIG(0) THEN FLAG=0:REPT=0:RETURN
5220  IF REPT THEN REPT=REPT-1:RETURN
5230  X=X(HEAD):Y=Y(HEAD)
5240  X1=AMX(TYPE):Y1=AMY(TYPE)
5250  X1=X1+X:IF X1<0 OR X1>39 THEN RETURN
5260  Y1=Y1+Y:IF Y1<0 OR Y1>22 THEN RETURN
5270  CHANGE=1
5280  HEAD=HEAD-1
5290  IF HEAD<0 THEN HEAD=970
5300  X(HEAD)=X1:Y(HEAD)=Y1
5310  IF  NOT FLAG THEN REPT=6:FLAG=1
5320  RETURN
```

Random number to screen

```
6000    Z=INT(RND(0)*9)+17:IF TAIL=HEAD AND Z=17 THEN 6000
6010    POST=INT(RND(0)*920)+SCREEN
6020    IF PEEK(POST) THEN 6010
6030    TEST=1
6040    POKE POST,Z
6050    RETURN
```

End of game

```
10000   GRAPHICS 2+16
10010   ? #6;"SCORE :";SCORE
10020   ? #6
10030   ? #6
10040   ? #6;"PRESS <RETURN>"
10050   POKE 754,255
10060   IF PEEK(754)<>12 THEN 10060
10070   CLR :GOTO 10
```

Initialize

```
20000   BODY=84
20010   DIM FRONT(3)
20020   FRONT(0)=92:FRONT(1)=93:FRONT(2)=94:FRONT(3)=95
20040   DIM AMX(3),AMY(3)
20050   AMX(0)=0:AMY(0)=-1
20060   AMX(1)=0:AMY(1)=1
20070   AMX(2)=-1:AMY(2)=0
20080   AMX(3)=1:AMY(3)=0
20090   TYPE=0
20100   SCORE=0
20110   TEST=0
20120   SCREEN=40000
20130   DIM X(970),Y(970)
20140   X(0)=19:Y(0)=12
20150   HEAD=0:TAIL=0:DROP=0:REPEAT=0:TYPE=0
20160   ? CHR$(125)
20170   GOTO 100
```

ChexSum Tables

```
   10 = 549            5210 = 976         10050 = 407
  100 = 1972           5220 = 835         10060 = 701
  110 = 1406           5230 = 1324        10070 = 180
  120 = 1056           5240 = 1397        20000 = 474
  130 = 2845           5250 = 1355        20010 = 374
  140 = 1744           5260 = 1341        20020 = 2832
  150 = 916            5270 = 347         20040 = 742
  160 = 1249           5280 = 514         20050 = 979
  170 = 1292           5290 = 704         20060 = 1054
  180 = 1763           5300 = 1329        20070 = 1111
  181 = 596            5310 = 989         20080 = 1058
  190 = 1616           5320 = 56          20090 = 286
  200 = 447            6000 = 1837        20100 = 280
  210 = 1174           6010 = 985         20110 = 281
  220 = 112            6020 = 580         20120 = 345
 5000 = 471            6030 = 346         20130 = 938
 5010 = 502            6040 = 381         20140 = 988
 5020 = 3174           6050 = 58          20150 = 1590
 5030 = 502           10000 = 282         20160 = 343
 5040 = 569           10010 = 853         20170 = 112
 5050 = 567           10020 = 174
 5060 = 568           10030 = 174
 5200 = 282           10040 = 1255        TOTAL = 58541
```

PATROL CAR

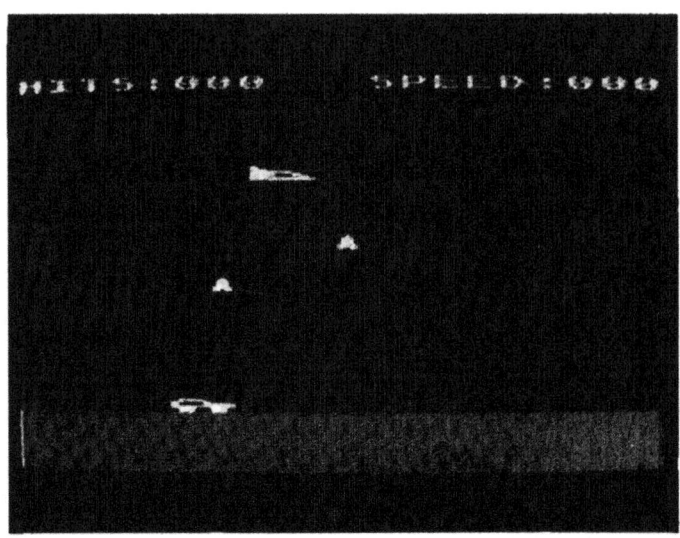

CLASSIFICATION: Arcade

Move your little patrol car along the ground and shoot down the hostile invaders and their missiles. Use the joystick to move left and right and the fire button to launch missiles. The aliens can drop nasties on you so beware!!!!

PROGRAMMING SUGGESTIONS

Add obstacles to your patrol cars path to make hitting the alien more difficult. Make it possible for several invaders to attack you at the same time.

Program Variables

X1	X position of patrol car
Y1	Y position of patrol car
A	Joystick variable
X3	X position of alien
Y3	Y position of alien
X2	X position of his missile
Y2	Y position of his missile
X4	X position of your missile
Y4	Y position of your missile

Program Structure

5 -	85	Set up players and draw screen
100 -	130	Data for shapes
1060 -	1560	Main loop
2000 -	2210	Move the patrol car
3000 -	3010	Move the alien
4000 -	4499	Move his missile
5000 -	5999	Move your missile
7000 -	7999	Collision checking

Listing

```
5       FOR I=33792 TO 33792+1023:POKE I,0:NEXT I
6       FOR I=30720 TO 30796:READ A:POKE I,A:NEXT I
7       FOR I=28672 TO 29050:READ A:POKE I,A:NEXT I
10      POKE 106,128
20      PM=PEEK(106):PMBASE=PM*256
30      GRAPHICS 1
40      POKE 559,62
50      POKE 53277,3
60      POKE 54279,PM
70      POKE 53256,2
80      POKE 704,77:POKE 705,77:POKE 706,77
85      POKE 707,77
100     DATA 0,0,112,136,135,255,102,102,0,0,0,0,0,0,0,0,0,0,0,0,
        0
110     DATA 16,56,56,56,124,108,0,0,0,0,0,0,0,0,0,0,0,0,0,0,0,
        0,0
120     DATA 128,192,248,228,226,255,255,124,0,0,0,0,0,0,0,0,0
130     DATA 16,56,56,56,124,108,0,0,0,0,0,0,0,0,0,0,0
200     POKE 53256,1
210     POKE 53257,2
220     POKE 53258,1
230     POKE 53259,2
500     X3=0:GOSUB 4500:Y3=Y
505     X1=50:Y1=153
1030    A=USR(28672,X1,Y1,X2,Y2,X3,Y3,X4,Y4)
1060    POSITION 0,0:PRINT #6;"HITS:";HI;" ▄BANGS:";BA;" ▄▄";
1500    GOSUB 2000:REM PATROL CAR
1510    GOSUB 3000:REM ALIEN
1520    GOSUB 4000:REM HIS MISSILE
1530    GOSUB 5000:REM YOUR MISSILE
1545    A=USR(112*256,X1,Y1,X2,Y2,X3,Y3,X4,Y4)
1550    GOSUB 7000:REM CHECK
1560    GOTO 1060
2000    REM
2010    POKE 53278,0:A=STICK(1):IF A=15 THEN RETURN
2020    IF A=11 THEN GOSUB 2100
2030    IF A=7 THEN GOSUB 2200
2040    IF STRIG(1)=0 THEN 5500:RETURN
2050    RETURN
2100    REM
2105    IF X1<3 THEN RETURN
2110    X1=X1-4:RETURN
2200    REM
2205    IF X1>140 THEN RETURN
2210    X1=X1+4:RETURN
3000    REM
3005    IF X3>163 THEN GOSUB 4500:Y3=Y:X3=0:RETURN
3010    X3=X3+5:RETURN
4000    REM
4005    IF IT1=0 THEN GOSUB 4100
4010    IF Y2>155 THEN IT1=0:HI=HI+1:Y2=220:RETURN
4020    Y2=Y2+4
4025    IF X2>140 THEN RETURN
4030    X2=X2+4:RETURN
4100    X2=X3:Y2=Y3+8:IT1=1:RETURN
```

```
4499 RETURN
4500 Y=INT(RND(1)*120):IF Y<8 THEN 4500
4505 RETURN
5000 REM
5003 IF IT2=0 THEN RETURN
5005 IF Y4<8 THEN IT2=0:Y4=220:RETURN
5010 Y4=Y4-4:RETURN
5500 IF IT2=1 THEN RETURN
5505 X4=X1:Y4=Y1-8:IT2=1:RETURN
5999 RETURN
7000 REM
7010 IF PEEK(53261)=1 THEN BA=BA-1:IT1=0:Y2=220
7020 IF PEEK(53263)=2 THEN BA=BA+1
7030 IF PEEK(53263)=4 THEN BA=BA+1
7999 RETURN
9000 DATA 104,104,104,141,61,113,104,104,141,60,113,104,104,
     141,75,113,104,104,141,74
9005 DATA 113,104,104,141,89,113,104,104,141,88,113,104,104,
     141,103,113,104,104,141,102
9010 DATA 113,32,45,112,96,120,32,8,113,160,14,162,0,189,53,
     113,149,176,232,136
9015 DATA 208,247,32,170,112,160,14,162,0,181,176,157,53,113
     ,232,136,208,247,160,14
9020 DATA 162,0,189,67,113,149,176,232,136,208,247,32,170,11
     2,160,14,162,0,181,176
9025 DATA 157,67,113,232,136,208,247,160,14,162,0,189,81,113
     ,149,176,232,136,208,247
9030 DATA 32,170,112,160,14,162,0,181,176,157,81,113,232,136
     ,208,247,160,14,162,0
9035 DATA 189,95,113,149,176,232,136,208,247,32,170,112,160,
     14,162,0,181,176,157,95
9040 DATA 113,232,136,208,247,32,22,113,88,96,165,183,197,18
     2,240,68,160,0,165,184
9045 DATA 24,105,46,145,176,169,32,24,101,182,168,166,185,16
     9,0,145,178,200,202,16
9050 DATA 250,169,32,24,101,183,141,116,113,162,0,142,109,11
     3,166,185,172,109,113,177
9055 DATA 180,238,109,113,172,116,113,145,178,238,116,113,20
     2,16,237,165,183,133,182,165
9060 DATA 184,133,189,96,165,184,197,189,208,182,96,173,112,
     113,41,15,170,189,36,113
9065 DATA 238,112,113,96,160,14,162,0,181,176,157,117,113,23
     2,136,208,247,96,160,14
9070 DATA 162,0,189,117,113,149,176,232,136,208,247,96,1,2,3
     ,4,5,10,7,8
9075 DATA 7,8,11,4,2,4,1,4,8,0,208,0,132,0,120,0,0,0,8,0
9080 DATA 16,0,0,1,208,0,133,20,120,0,0,0,8,0,16,0,0,2,208,0
9085 DATA 134,40,120,0,0,0,8,0,16,0,0,3,208,0,135,60,120,0,0
     ,0
9090 DATA 8,0,0,0,0,0,0,79,0,0,0,0,0,0,0,141,30,208
```

ChexSum Tables

5 = 1421	1530 = 1275	5500 = 367
6 = 1353	1545 = 2286	5505 = 1408
7 = 1627	1550 = 749	5999 = 58
10 = 277	1560 = 223	7010 = 1869
20 = 1124	2010 = 1338	7020 = 1113
30 = 144	2020 = 463	7030 = 1115
40 = 420	2030 = 454	7999 = 58
50 = 406	2040 = 624	9000 = 3800
60 = 473	2050 = 58	9005 = 3900
70 = 372	2105 = 358	9010 = 3548
80 = 1169	2110 = 587	9015 = 3747
85 = 361	2205 = 422	9020 = 3711
100 = 2569	2210 = 586	9025 = 3824
110 = 2668	3005 = 1412	9030 = 3638
120 = 2534	3010 = 581	9035 = 3778
130 = 2116	4005 = 428	9040 = 3730
200 = 371	4010 = 1768	9045 = 3719
210 = 373	4020 = 516	9050 = 3845
220 = 373	4025 = 424	9055 = 4013
230 = 375	4030 = 590	9060 = 3852
500 = 889	4100 = 1396	9065 = 3760
505 = 859	4499 = 58	9070 = 3163
1030 = 2315	4500 = 1341	9075 = 2355
1060 = 1692	4505 = 58	9080 = 2537
1500 = 1036	5003 = 302	9085 = 2637
1510 = 696	5005 = 1107	9090 = 2191
1520 = 1151	5010 = 597	

TOTAL = 120901

ROBOTS

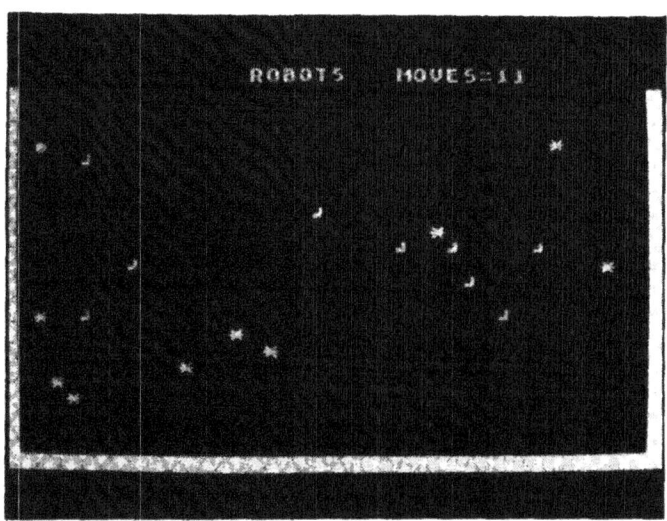

CLASSIFICATION: Skill

The objective of this game is to move your player round the screen without being destroyed by the robots. Each time you move, all the robots move toward you. You can destroy the robots by causing them to walk over mines which you must avoid yourself. Select a joystick at the start of the game. Try to destroy all the robots in the least number of moves.

PROGRAMMING SUGGESTIONS

Increase the number of robots and mines on the screen. Place obstacles on the screen to make moving more difficult.

Program Variables

MO	Number of moves
SP	Space character
NR	Number of robots
PL	Players character
NM	Number of mines
JO	Joystick port number
SC	Start of screen

Program Structure

```
 120 -  180   Main Loop
1000 - 1099   Initialization
2000 - 2099   Setup game, input joystick number
3000 - 3030   Deposit mines
4000 - 4040   Deposit robots
5000 - 5030   Move player
6000 - 6020   Move player right
6100 - 6120   Move player left
```

Listing

```
10      REM ROBOTS
20      CLR
21      POKE 752,255
40      SC=40000
60      GOSUB 1000:REM INITIALIZE VARAIABLE
70      GOSUB 2000:REM DO INSTRUCTIONS
80      GOSUB 3000:REM DEPOIST MINES
90      GOSUB 4000:REM DEPOSIT DROIDS
100     GOSUB 5000:REM DEPOSIT PLAYER
```

```
                    Main Loop
```

```
120     A=STICK(JO):B=STRIG(JO):IF A=15 AND B=1 THEN 120
130     IF A=7 THEN GOSUB 6000
140     IF A=11 THEN GOSUB 6100
150     IF A=13 THEN GOSUB 6200
160     IF A=14 THEN GOSUB 6300
165     POSITION 0,0:PRINT SPC$(1,30);MO;
170     IF B=0 THEN POKE PO,SP:GOSUB 5000
180     GOSUB 8000:GOTO 120
```

```
                 Initialization
```

```
1000    SETCOLOR 4,7,5:SETCOLOR 2,3,6:SETCOLOR 1,3,15
1010    DIM TAB(10,2),E(10),SPC$(40)
1020    NM=10:REM SET NUMBER OF MINES
1025    PL=84:REM SET PLAYER CHAR
1030    ROB=67
1035    MIN=10:REM SET MINE CHAR
1040    NR=10:REM SET NUMBER OF ROBOTS
1050    SP=0:REM SET SP CHARACTER
1060    EX=17
1070    FOR I=1 TO 40:SPC$(I,I)="→":NEXT I
1099    RETURN
```

```
2000    POKE 752,0
2026    POKE 752,0
2027    PRINT CHR$(125);"WHICH JOYSTICK PORT (0,1)";:INPUT JO
2028    IF JO<>0 AND JO<>1 THEN 2027
2029    PRINT CHR$(125);:POKE 752,128
2030    FOR I=SC+1 TO SC+39:POKE I+920,128:NEXT I
2040    FOR I=SC+40 TO SC+920 STEP 40:POKE I,128:POKE I+39,128:
        NEXT I
2050    POKE SC,128
2060    POKE SC+920,128:POKE SC+920+39,128
2070    POSITION 0,0:PRINT "▲▲▲▲▲▲▲▲▲▲▲▲▲▲▲▲▲ROBOTS▲▲▲
        MOVES=0▲▲▲▲▲▲▲▲▲";
        2099   RETURN
```

```
Deposit mines
```

```
3000    FOR I=1 TO NM
3007    RW=INT(RND(0)*23):IF RW=0 THEN 3007
3010    CW=INT(RND(0)*39):IF CW=0 THEN 3010
3020    PE=SC+(RW*40)+CW
3025    IF PEEK(PE)=MIN THEN 3007
3030    POKE PE,MIN:NEXT I:RETURN
```

```
Deposit robots
```

```
4000    FOR I=1 TO NR
4007    E(I)=1
4010    RW=INT(RND(0)*23):IF RW=0 THEN 4010
4015    CW=INT(RND(0)*39):IF CW=0 THEN 4015
4020    PE=SC+(RW*40)+CW
4025    IF PEEK(PE)=MIN THEN 4010
4030    IF PEEK(PE)=ROB THEN 4010
4035    TAB(I,1)=RW:TAB(I,2)=CW
4040    POKE PE,ROB
4050    NEXT I
4060    RETURN
```

```
5000  R=INT(RND(0)*23):IF R=0 THEN 5000
5010  C=INT(RND(0)*39):IF C=0 THEN 5010
5015  PO=SC+(R*40)+C
5020  IF PEEK(PO)=MIN THEN 5000
5025  IF PEEK(PO)=ROB THEN 5000
5030  MO=MO+5:POKE PO,PL:RETURN
6000  REM MOVE PLAYER RIGHT
6005  IF C=38 THEN RETURN
6006  MO=MO+1
6007  C=C+1:PE=SC+(R*40)+C
6010  IF PEEK(PE)=ROB THEN GOSUB 9000:GOTO 10
6012  IF PEEK(PE)=MIN THEN GOSUB 9500:GOTO 10
6020  POKE PO,SP:POKE PE,PL:PO=PE:RETURN
6100  REM MOVE PLAYER LEFT
6105  IF C=1 THEN RETURN
6106  MO=MO+1
6107  C=C-1:PE=SC+(R*40)+C
6110  IF PEEK(PE)=ROB THEN GOSUB 9000:GOTO 10
6112  IF PEEK(PE)=MIN THEN GOSUB 9500:GOTO 10
6120  POKE PO,SP:POKE PE,PL:PO=PE:RETURN
6200  REM MOVE PLAYER DOWN
6205  IF R=22 THEN RETURN
6206  MO=MO+1
6207  R=R+1:PE=SC+(R*40)+C
6210  IF PEEK(PE)=ROB THEN GOSUB 9000:GOTO 10
6212  IF PEEK(PE)=MIN THEN GOSUB 9500:GOTO 10
6220  POKE PO,SP:POKE PE,PL:PO=PE:RETURN
6300  REM MOVE PLAYER UP
6305  IF R=1 THEN RETURN
6306  MO=MO+1
6307  R=R-1:PE=SC+(R*40)+C
6310  IF PEEK(PE)=ROB THEN GOSUB 9000:GOTO 10
6312  IF PEEK(PE)=MIN THEN GOSUB 9500:GOTO 10
6320  POKE PO,SP:POKE PE,PL:PO=PE:RETURN
8000  REM MOVE ROBOTS
8020  CC=0:FOR I=1 TO NR
8030  IF E(I)=1 THEN GOSUB 8500:CC=CC+1
8040  NEXT I
8050  IF CC=0 THEN GOSUB 9900:GOTO 10
8060  RETURN
8500  REM MOVE ONE ROBOT
8505  RW=TAB(I,1):CW=TAB(I,2):PE=SC+(RW*40)+CW
8520  IF CW<C THEN TC=CW:TC=TC+1
8525  IF CW>C THEN TC=CW:TC=TC-1
8530  IF RW<R THEN TR=RW:TR=TR+1
8535  IF RW>R THEN TR=RW:TR=TR-1
8540  PN=SC+(TR*40)+TC
8545  IF PEEK(PN)=MIN THEN POKE PN,SP:POKE PE,SP:E(I)=0:RETUR
      N
8550  IF PEEK(PN)=ROB THEN RETURN
8560  IF PEEK(PN)=PL THEN GOSUB 9000:GOTO 10
8570  TAB(I,1)=TR:TAB(I,2)=TC:POKE PE,SP:POKE PN,ROB:RETURN
9000  REM THE ROBOTS GOT YOU
9005  PRINT CHR$(125);:PRINT "YOU WERE CAPTURED BY THE
       ROBOTS !!!!!"
9010  PRINT :PRINT "YOU MADE ";MO;" MOVES"
9012  CC=0:FOR I=1 TO NR:IF E(I)=0 THEN CC=CC+1
9013  NEXT I
9015  PRINT :PRINT "AND DESTROYED ";CC;" ROBOTS"
```

```
9020  GOSUB 10000:RETURN
9500  REM PLAYER HIT A MINE
9505  PRINT CHR$(125);"YOU HIT A SUBATOMIC MINE"
9510  PRINT :PRINT "YOUR MOLOCULES ARE NOW ORBITING THE"
9512  CC=0:FOR I=1 TO NR:IF E(I)=0 THEN CC=CC+1
9513  NEXT I
9515  PRINT :PRINT "EARTH!!!!!":PRINT
9520  PRINT "YOU MADE ";MO;" MOVES":PRINT
9525  PRINT "AND DESTROYED ";CC;" ROBOTS":GOSUB 10000:RETURN
9900  REM ALL ROBOTS GONE
9905  PRINT CHR$(125);"YOU HAVE DESTROYED ALL THE ROBOTS":
      PRINT
9910  PRINT "IT TOOK YOU ";MO;" MOVES":PRINT
9915  GOSUB 10000:GOTO 10
10000 PRINT :PRINT "PRESS JOYSTICK TRIGGER TO RESTART GAME"
10005 B=STRIG(JO):IF B=1 THEN 10005
10010 RETURN
```

ChexSum Tables

```
  20 = 40          3020 = 1026       6310 = 962
  21 = 405         3025 = 684        6312 = 968
  40 = 333         3030 = 617        6320 = 1211
  60 = 1751        4000 = 465        8020 = 777
  70 = 1457        4007 = 581        8030 = 1379
  80 = 1291        4010 = 1240       8040 = 175
  90 = 1381        4015 = 1269       8050 = 682
 100 = 1405        4020 = 1026       8060 = 58
 120 = 1916        4025 = 709        8505 = 2688
 130 = 516         4030 = 708        8520 = 1360
 140 = 527         4035 = 1607       8525 = 1362
 150 = 530         4040 = 358        8530 = 1360
 160 = 532         4050 = 175        8535 = 1362
 165 = 881         4060 = 58         8540 = 1044
 170 = 796         5000 = 1246       8545 = 1937
 180 = 406         5010 = 1286       8550 = 606
1000 = 1204        5015 = 1019       8560 = 967
1010 = 1258        5020 = 696        8570 = 2532
1020 = 1861        5025 = 695        9005 = 2855
1025 = 1703        5030 = 954        9010 = 1379
1030 = 442         6005 = 427        9012 = 1877
1035 = 1423        6006 = 503        9013 = 175
1040 = 1959        6007 = 1602       9015 = 1857
1050 = 1573        6010 = 962        9020 = 187
1060 = 365         6012 = 968        9505 = 2046
1070 = 1460        6020 = 1211       9510 = 2679
1099 = 58          6105 = 372        9512 = 1877
2000 = 253         6106 = 503        9513 = 175
2026 = 253         6107 = 1603       9515 = 765
2027 = 2256        6110 = 962        9520 = 1379
2028 = 661         6112 = 968        9525 = 2028
2029 = 748         6120 = 1211       9905 = 2822
2030 = 1549        6205 = 404        9910 = 1612
2040 = 2200        6206 = 503        9915 = 262
2050 = 319         6207 = 1600      10000 = 2915
2060 = 1173        6210 = 962       10005 = 984
2070 = 2114        6212 = 968       10010 = 58
2099 = 58          6220 = 1211
3000 = 461         6305 = 371
3007 = 1215        6306 = 503       TOTAL = 127177
3010 = 1248        6307 = 1601
```

You may also enjoy...

Printed in Great Britain
by Amazon

ChexSum Tables

```
20   = 40            3020 = 1026         6310  = 962
21   = 405           3025 = 684          6312  = 968
40   = 333           3030 = 617          6320  = 1211
60   = 1751          4000 = 465          8020  = 777
70   = 1457          4007 = 581          8030  = 1379
80   = 1291          4010 = 1240         8040  = 175
90   = 1381          4015 = 1269         8050  = 682
100  = 1405          4020 = 1026         8060  = 58
120  = 1916          4025 = 709          8505  = 2688
130  = 516           4030 = 708          8520  = 1360
140  = 527           4035 = 1607         8525  = 1362
150  = 530           4040 = 358          8530  = 1360
160  = 532           4050 = 175          8535  = 1362
165  = 881           4060 = 58           8540  = 1044
170  = 796           5000 = 1246         8545  = 1937
180  = 406           5010 = 1286         8550  = 606
1000 = 1204          5015 = 1019         8560  = 967
1010 = 1258          5020 = 696          8570  = 2532
1020 = 1861          5025 = 695          9005  = 2855
1025 = 1703          5030 = 954          9010  = 1379
1030 = 442           6005 = 427          9012  = 1877
1035 = 1423          6006 = 503          9013  = 175
1040 = 1959          6007 = 1602         9015  = 1857
1050 = 1573          6010 = 962          9020  = 187
1060 = 365           6012 = 968          9505  = 2046
1070 = 1460          6020 = 1211         9510  = 2679
1099 = 58            6105 = 372          9512  = 1877
2000 = 253           6106 = 503          9513  = 175
2026 = 253           6107 = 1603         9515  = 765
2027 = 2256          6110 = 962          9520  = 1379
2028 = 661           6112 = 968          9525  = 2028
2029 = 748           6120 = 1211         9905  = 2822
2030 = 1549          6205 = 404          9910  = 1612
2040 = 2200          6206 = 503          9915  = 262
2050 = 319           6207 = 1600         10000 = 2915
2060 = 1173          6210 = 962          10005 = 984
2070 = 2114          6212 = 968          10010 = 58
2099 = 58            6220 = 1211
3000 = 461           6305 = 371
3007 = 1215          6306 = 503          TOTAL = 127177
3010 = 1248          6307 = 1601
```

You may also enjoy...